HEALING FROM THE HEART

A POWERFUL COLLECTION OF INSPIRATIONAL LIFE STORIES

TRIBE CALLED SUCCESS   NALEIGHNA KAI

STEPHANIE M. FREEMAN   RANDI COLEY

BRIDGETT MCGILL   U. M. HIRAM

DANIELLE FRANKLIN DETIEGE   LA AMMITAI

CATHY A. BROWN   YVONNE ELLIOTT

KAREN GLAPION STAMPLEY

Foreword by
PAT G'ORGE-WALKER
Foreword by
MARY MONROE

MACRO PUBLISHING GROUP

.

Ebook ISBN: 978-1-952871-84-9

Trade Paperback ISBN: 978-1-952871-85-6

Cover designed by J. L. Woodson for Woodson Creative Studio

Interior Design: Lissa Woodson for Woodson Creative Studio

Editing by Ellen Kiley Goeckler, Naleighna Kai, and Stephanie M. Freeman

TRIGGER WARNING NOTE FROM THE CURATOR

Thank you for taking this journey into the lives of 10 amazing women. Please note, these are real life accounts and just a few delve into sensitive and painful experiences with mentions of domestic violence and assault. I ask that you keep this in mind as you move forward.

_Naleighna Kai

FOREWORD BY MARY MONROE

Not every Black woman has been mistreated but I am sure we all know some who have. Books on this subject, fiction and non-fiction, have inspired and stimulated me for years. I know first-hand how devastating abuse can be, so this anthology will be one of the most important books in my personal library.

I was three-years-old the first time I witnessed abuse in my family. Mom was pregnant with my half-sister. My stepfather, an alcoholic who could never keep a job, spent his days and nights drinking and chasing women. I had an older sister and brother and we all had to work on farms to help Mom pay our household expenses. She also worked on the farms when she couldn't find work cleaning houses. One day when she returned from the grocery store, my delusional stepfather accused her of having an affair with the elderly man who had given her a ride home. He staggered up to her and began to pummel her with his fists. Afterwards, Mom bandaged her wounds, cooked dinner, and acted like nothing had happened. The violence eventually began to happen so often, I thought it was part of being married. When I played house with my five-year-old male neighbor who played the role of my husband, part of the game was that he was allowed to punch and slap me whenever he felt like it. He never hit hard enough to hurt me, and afterwards we'd continue playing as if nothing had happened. When my mother fought back, it only made my stepfather more violent. I never fought back, even years later when my beatings became the real thing.

I witnessed a lot of violence against other women I knew. The meek, kind-hearted woman next door was attacked by her husband on a regular basis. My older teenage sister would go out with her jealous boyfriend and come home with black eyes and other bruises. The list of examples involving other women is very long.

I was surprised when another woman I knew finally ended her abuse. Her husband, a well-respected deacon in our church, had treated her like a queen before she married him. She didn't know that he had a dark side. Shortly after their wedding, he began to beat her and flaunt his other women. He found out too late that his wife also had a dark side. After only a couple of years of abuse, that woman fought back one day with an eight-inch butcher knife. Three days after her husband's funeral, the district attorney decided it was a clear case of self-defense and declined to prosecute. She has been happily married to her second husband for over twenty-five years.

There was another woman in my neighborhood who bragged that she had never been abused or disrespected by her husband. She was very independent and successful in everything she did. Because her husband didn't control her, he was called a sissy behind his back. One day I asked her why her husband allowed her to have so much freedom. First, she looked at me like I was speaking in tongues. And then she replied, "*Allowed?* That man don't own me so it ain't up to him to allow me to do nothing! *I* allow myself to do whatever I want. No man has the right to control a woman's life." I am happy to report that I knew a few other women like her.

I was a nosy youngster. One day I asked one of my aunts why she had never left my abusive uncle. Her exact words were, "Black men have been beaten down so much by The Man, they have to do something to make themselves feel like men. Their women are the safest ones to take out their frustrations on. We don't want their self-esteem to get any lower so we learn to live with their bad behavior." I decided right then and there that I was not going to "live with bad behavior."

However, when I got married at age nineteen, my husband told me on our wedding night that he was in charge of every move I made. He warned me that each time I stepped out of line, he would beat me like I'd "stole something." The first time was only a few weeks later when I went to a nearby store to pick up a few items for dinner. Before I'd left the house he'd told me, "You'd better be back here in fifteen minutes or I'm going to make you regret it!" Well, the store was crowded and I was not able to be back home in fifteen minutes. Just as the cashier began to ring up my items, I heard a commotion outside. When I turned around to see who was doing all the loud cussing, I was horrified to see the man I'd recently married standing in the doorway with his thick leather belt in his hand. He stormed in and gave me several lashes and accused me of lollygagging so I could flirt with some of the male customers. I was pregnant at the time but I started making plans to end my marriage as soon as I could. Unfortunately, he derailed my plans when he promised me that he would change. He didn't.

I found solace in reading and writing fiction. My husband didn't want me to do anything he didn't approve of, and at the top of his list were reading and writing. He volunteered me to babysit his friends' unruly kids for free, iron large bushels of clothes for his mother, and even keep his grandmother's house clean. I didn't want to move back home and I didn't have a job, so I was trapped. My spouse decided that the publications I read and the soap operas I watched about people having affairs would give me ideas.

He told me I could no longer do either one. I still watched the TV shows I liked, read, and wrote when he was not at home. He didn't know that I sold stories to some of the romance magazines I had been reading since middle school. One day he beat me to our mailbox. He opened a letter addressed to me from one of the magazine publishers that contained an acceptance letter and the payment for one of my stories. He hit the roof, tore up the manuscript I'd been working on, and told me that my "writing foolishness" was over. However, when I cashed the check, that slimy devil took half of the money.

I continued to write whenever I was alone in the house. I stored my manuscripts-in-progress in a box and hid them in my neighbor's basement. I put in a change-of-address request so that my mail from the magazine publishers would go to my mother's house. Writing was and still is my lifeline. There was no way on earth I was going to let someone take away something that meant so much to me.

I was pregnant with my second child and had a black eye and other bruises when I finally decided I'd suffered enough. The man who had vowed to love and honor me had slapped me because I'd had a "stupid look" on my face. I found out after I'd left him that he and one of my closest friends had been having an affair for months and she was also pregnant with his child.

The next man in my life promised to protect me from my ex. He supported me financially, (my ex refused to pay spousal and child support) so I moved one town over and started a serious relationship with my "protector." Lo and behold, he turned out to be more violent and controlling than the man I'd married! He wouldn't let me visit my friends unless he went with me. I couldn't watch certain TV shows. I was not allowed to wear provocative clothes, smile at other men, and the only publication I was allowed to read was the Bible. Yes, he called himself a Christian. After one violent episode, he made a noose out of a towel and threatened to hang me the next time I made him angry. Even a little thing like "missing a spot" when I mopped a floor made him mad so, once again, I had to walk on egg shells in my own home.

Writing made life so much easier for me during those dark days. I spent as much time as possible creating characters and putting them in outrageous situations before easing their pain. It was very therapeutic. But things eventually blew up in my face. The man I was involved with decided he wasn't going to allow me to continue "scribbling stories" and "fiddling around on a type-writer" because he thought that I should have been catering to him more. He thought it was a joke that I had the nerve to want to become a successful author and assured me that I was wasting my time. According to him, I couldn't write a grocery list, let alone a publishable novel (he had never read any of my work). That was the straw that broke the camel's back. I finally decided that I had to flee an environment that had become completely unbearable.

When I told my family that I was leaving Ohio and moving to California, they told me I was too countrified to make it in such a sophisticated and fast-paced state. One cousin even advised me to go back to the man I'd exchanged vows with because at least he had a good job and he had become a "changed" man...again. I packed my suitcase anyway and purchased a one-way ticket to Richmond, California where my mother's sister lived. The brutal boyfriend I had left had been stalking me and threatening to teach me a lesson I'd never forget. I was so terrified, I had to sneak to the Greyhound bus station before dawn on a cold day in January.

I stayed with my aunt for three weeks before I found a job and my own apartment. It wasn't what I wanted, but I had never felt so liberated and empowered in my life. I was determined to reclaim my life and become a successful author.

My last abuser had indeed "taught me a lesson I'd never forget." I learned that with faith and determination I could be in a relationship and not have to endure abuse. But I had to be strong enough to remove myself from a bad situation before it got worse. My next few relationships with men were casual because I needed to focus on my two toddlers and pursue more vigorously my life-long dream to become a successful author. Despite my last abuser's claim that I couldn't write a publishable book, my first mentor, iconic author *Toni Morrison,* edited some of my work. She predicted that someday I would exceed my expectations if I worked hard enough and never gave up.

I worked days as a secretary at a large engineering firm in San Francisco and wrote for hours after supper; sometimes until it was time for me to get ready for work the next morning. Despite the hundreds of rejection letters I received from literary agents and publishers, I continued to write and tell myself, "As long as I keep trying, I have a chance to succeed." A few mean agents and editors told me I would never publish a book. Those words hurt almost as much as the physical and verbal abuse I'd endured in my back-to-back nightmares. They also motivated me.

After I'd been in California for a couple of years, I realized how strong I had become. Each time a man attempted to control me I *immediately* ended the relationship. But most of the new men in my life were very good to me.

My abusers in Ohio had never attacked me in front of my children. In our new location, they witnessed abuse in the homes of some of their friends. I made it clear to them that it was not acceptable and should never be tolerated. They rolled their eyes when I told them what I'd gone through. They accused me of exaggerating because it was hard for them to believe that a woman like me had ever put up with an abusive man.

I took Toni Morrison's advice and worked harder and never gave up. She was right. I worked so hard that I am now the New York Times bestselling author of over thirty-five books. My most successful title, *Mrs. Wiggins,* is still selling well after its release in 2021. My second and third most successful books, *Mama Ruby* and *God Don't Like Ugly* were the #1 new releases on Amazon for several weeks. The women in my stories are composites of myself and other women I know. The one thing we all have in common is that we work hard and eventually succeed in almost everything we do. Some of my female characters are so scary and invincible, no man in his right mind would ever disrespect them. If you need proof, read these three: *Mrs. Wiggins*, *Mama Ruby* and *Bad Blood*.

I did a book signing in the Ohio town that I had fled and my ex-husband showed up. With a sheepish grin on his face, he told me, "You was so hardheaded when I had your crazy ass, I knew someday you'd get them books published." I actually thanked him for helping me make the decision to leave him, and I even gave him part of the credit for my success.

Faith and determination had sustained me. My bad experiences had actually been detours that eventually led me to success and peace of mind. After a few detours of their own, both of my sisters and my two daughters experienced healthy relationships with their partners. My stepfather eventually drank himself to death. Mom's next husband treated her like a queen until she passed away many years later.

One thing that I do now when I begin a new relationship with a man is that I let them know before the game even starts what I will and will not tolerate. It has been decades since I took control of my life, and I'm still in control.

—Mary Monroe, New York Times Bestselling author of *God Don't Like Ugly, The Upper Room, Gonna Lay Down My Burdens, Can You Keep a Secret, Deliver Me From Evil,* and *Empty Vows*
Visit her on the web: marymonroe.org

INTRODUCTION BY PAT G'ORGE-WALKER

Imagine an Oprah Winfrey show audience. Many were overjoyed, especially when she pointed at them while saying, "You get a car. You get a car." The recipients went wild. Those who watched on television were happy and a bit envious. What those watching on television as well as the audience members did not know — the recipients paid taxes on the car before they drove away. So it came at an unexpected, and not quite noticeable cost.

Substitute that same scenario with the experience often felt during some people's lifetime, "You get trauma, and you get trauma."

Those watching may envy us because we rarely show what we have been through. Women, especially, have a talent when it comes to hiding the cost of our Alabaster Survival Box. Because we have concealed it so well: *attractively packaged in an existence of smiles, laughter and especially our 'go along to get along' attitude; or the "what happens in our house, stays in our house" warnings.* It is unsurprising that there is a reason many folks, including relatives, who see our survival never realize what it cost.

In the *Healing from the Heart* anthology, the theme, the heart-felt disclosure of the contributors become a much-needed balm for the open wounds, a cleansing for those feeling a bit of guilt because they survived—despite their trauma.

Using myself as an example.

Sexual Abuse: Been there. From the age of nine until twelve, I was at the mercy of a trusted uncle who destroyed my level of trust in adults, especially family.

Sexual Assault: Been there too. At the age of fifteen, left for dead in a wooded area of the Bronx, New York. Even today, in my seventies, I still remember the pain and fear. Even worse was the fact my father, the good reverend, would not report it to the police because it would "embarrass the family." So, I suffered with inner injuries to my body and my mind—again that feeling of not being worthy of basic protection. If I were not valuable to my father or uncle than what was my worth to anyone else?

Church Hurt: It was almost as bad as the previously mentioned offenses. I was nineteen years old and did not realize I had joined a cult. At the insistence of the church elders, I was married to a young man whom I had met three days prior. He was on his way to Viet Nam. It was a quick service in one of the church mother's apartments. Three weeks later he was on his way to Viet Nam and nine months later I was on my way to becoming a mother. I was not suited for either role. He was not either. It went on to become five years of both mental and physical abuse heaped upon me and our three children. I later went on to write about it in my book titled: "Choices." One quote summed it up perfectly. "Anna could not determine the day or the hour when she realized, and much worse, *accepted* her reality. She and her children had become the enemy in their home. Neither she nor her children knew the rules of a war they had not enlisted to fight."

Fortunately, God sent into my life my 'Jubilee husband.' A man who loved me and my children and made certain he was a help and not a hindrance to my emotional and physical being.

There is much more that could be told, but suffice it to say, I am a champion; and like the women who contributed to the "Healing from the Heart" anthology, our stories are diverse in experiences but in-sync with sharing some insight and wisdom to the blueprint of the Survivor-Warrior psyche.

With humbleness and sincerity, we unashamedly share our heartfelt examples of persistent healing methods in every word and on every page of this amazing book.

After all, We, Black Women, are the epitome of Black Steel.

Pat G'Orge-Walker
   National Bestselling Author of
   Fire in the Water and *Heaven Can Be Hell*

SURVIVING THE UNTHINKABLE
BY STEPHANIE M. FREEMAN

 Whispered Lie in the Dark

"I TOLD her I loved her to make her stop screaming," he said before lowering the lid to the dumpster.

Stomping on my head was their insurance. Fracturing my skull, eye socket and jaw were a bonus. Hiding my body in a dumpster increased their chances of no one finding out what they'd done. If I told anyone, that meant they would get in trouble. Parents found out and denied that their sons could ever do such a horrific thing. In the end, it would be my word against theirs and good church-going boys never lied.

The drug store was on my way home from school. I still had nine blocks to go before I saw the green awning at the center of the maze in my neighborhood. Rudy's always carried the best penny candy and the latest edition of my favorite heartthrob magazines a day earlier than other stores in the area. Miles, one of my brother's friends ran up to me in a panic.

"You have to come with me. It's Lucas, he's been hurt."

Miles was shorter than my brother, Lucas by a foot, but I didn't care. He was the first boy I had a crush on, so in my mind, he was perfect right down to the spray of freckles across his café au lait complexion and the dimple on his chin. The gap in his toothy smile always made me tingle inside. I was fourteen at the time and my curiosity in boys was just beginning to take shape. He was my brother's best friend and I trusted him completely.

Somehow, it never occurred to me to stop and call the police or an ambulance with the change in my coat pocket. I simply heard that my brother needed me. I dropped everything to follow. I had known that boy for years so surely, I could trust him, right? He'd help me and my brother once, right?

Nightmares follow me down into my sleep. Few come with shadows of monsters or vampires. Mine always start at the mouth of an alley that reeked of piss, vomit, and what I would later come to recognize as my own fear. The dreams ended at various stages or when my screams ripped me from sleep. Mercifully, all these years later, the screams are muted on the outside. On the inside, some part of me is still screaming. Four corners of a room are my haven. From there I can watch the door. From there, my mantra reminds me of who I am, how old I am and the simple fact that *I am safe*. And then, I hear my mother's voice.

Stay with me, Stephanie. Stay just a little while longer.

To this day, in my happiest and my darkest moments, I listen for my mother's voice.

Sometimes, a trip to the bathroom would push the reset button in my mind. Other times, the nightmares resumed in grisly detail. The snow looked orange under the streetlights. I remember thinking, *The snow is falling, and I am dying.*

I remember my brother's best friend whispering "I love you" over and over in my ear, and the way my hair and the world smelled of garbage. Some of the rats kept me warm while the others feasted. Sleep made sense... dying made even more sense with snatches of their conversation outside the dumpster still so close.

"Keep your story straight," one of them warned. "She can't tell if she's dead."

Most think death is a sudden thing and perhaps, for some, it is. A bolt of pain and then a growing darkness. Sometimes it is a sanity choking fear and then the nothingness of a forever kind of sleep. Maybe there is a pain that rises in octaves that blot out the sun. And then there are those that see it coming slowly, silently like a sigh moving over your skin like a thick blanket beckoning you to sleep.

Well-meaning people will tell you to put it behind you. Others may insist that you talk about it in fine detail to satisfy their morbid curiosity. My favorite was a college chum's boyfriend asking, "Did you like it?"

"He's hurt, Stephanie. You have to come with me,"

My older brother, Lucas—my nickname for him—lit up every room that he walked into. Charming and charismatic, my brother was easily a favorite among my family. Laughter was a song on continuous loop when my cousins joined us for sleepovers or continental breakfasts in the woods behind our grandmother's home. And there was Lucas at the helm holding court or telling stories and making up silly songs.

My brother was as big as a bear and just as ferocious when hurt. Miles had said so. I tried to keep calm as fearful images built in my mind. We passed several phone booths as my brother's best friend took me to rescue my brother from whatever tragedy had befallen him. I thought of calling my mother, but then I remembered the first aid class I took that summer and figured maybe I could help until someone else arrived. Surely, I would be safe with the boy who always shared a stick of gum, or half of a popsicle with me.

The further we moved into the alley the more my heart thumped in my chest. I searched the dimly lit area that bottle necked at one end and saw broken wooden milk crates and garbage. They blocked my exit. They smiled at me, but their eyes were dead. My question and my brother's name was muted on the first assailant's fist that slammed into me.

Screaming made them angry. Whenever I thought they were done another took their place. I remember the grit of the pavement digging into the side of my face and the musty smell of unwashed skin. Blood and sour water filled my mouth and nose as did other things before they were done. Biting made the beatings worse. I remember throwing up and how angry it made one of them as he launched a foot into my midsection for 'getting my filth' on his shoes.

The dumpster came last.

I still remember wanting to save my brother, not realizing I was the one that needed to be saved. My brother's friend stood there, holding the dumpster lid as the others tried to bury what they did. The blows had been continuous. After a while, even the cutting didn't hurt anymore. All I could think was to play dead. If I played well enough then maybe ... just maybe, they wouldn't hurt me anymore. Their conversation as they left me to die made it clear.

"Why'd you tell her you loved her?"

"Practice," Miles said, "I'm seeing my girl later."

Most of what I remember comes in flashes or impressions. The rest is filled with snatches of conversations and my mother and brother's recounts. My assailants even had the audacity to help my family search for me. Miles even came to the hospital and sat in the waiting room and stopped by for a visit, leaving my favorite penny candy and a blue and green stuffed turtle on the foot of my bed.

Many years later he took his own life and the others either turned to drugs and alcohol or were flushed away in the prison system and never seen again.

My own fate? Well, that was another story entirely.

The Living Doll Speaks

MOST PARENTS REMEMBER their child's first words. I clearly remember what I said when I learned to speak the second time. You see, my mother left me in the kitchen while she went to take care of something in another part of the house. She didn't realize she had been gone too long. The words felt like stones in my mouth when I first spoke and then yelled them . . .

Mom, the bacon is burning.

Mom came and stood at the threshold of the kitchen with tears streaming down her cheeks. She didn't care about the bacon. Her fourteen-year-old daughter had spoken her first words after nearly a year of taking care of what amounted to a living doll.

When they finally found me, I was more dead than alive, the doctor's made that clear. Every once in a while, my mother would recount the story of my life and near death experience.

I'll never forget it. They sat me down in a chair and kept patting my hand. They kept saying that I needed to pick out the clothes I would bury you in because you wouldn't ... no, couldn't, survive the night. I wasn't there when they found you half frozen. You were so quiet ... so broken. They had cleaned you up and covered you in blankets, but they kept insisting that with the extent of your injuries I needed to prepare myself.

I started laughing. They looked at me as if I had lost my mind. Maybe I did. I mean when you're pregnant, you make all of these bargains with God. You promise to be a good parent and you try to be. I tried to be. But with your father gone, it was just me and I had to work to keep a roof over our heads.

I never wanted you and your brother to be latchkey children, but what choice did I have? But then I saw you. Your brother came unglued. He started screaming so loud they had to sedate him. There were so many tubes running in and out of you, but I knew. I dried my face and looked that doctor straight in the eye and said, "You don't know the God I serve."

You were little more than a living doll when I finally brought you home. You didn't talk and you couldn't sit up on your own. When it rained, your head would hurt so bad, and your nose would bleed. They were convinced that the skull fracture and the broken eye socket would never heal properly. They were wrong. Even the gashes to your arm and leg from the box cutter faded for the most part.

Maybe it was selfish my asking you to stay. I knew you would never be my little girl anymore. How could you be? They'd hurt you so badly. But you see, I knew. I didn't care what those doctors said.

Everyone had an opinion about what I should do with you. Some made it plain enough. They wanted me to squirrel you away in some psych ward like a dirty little secret. Like you were somehow at fault, or something to be swept under the rug and forgotten. They made it sound like you were too damaged to live without being a vegetable or swaddled in a strait jacket the rest of your life.

But you were my baby. Mine. And I knew you were supposed to be here. No matter how many setbacks . . . I knew.

My mother spent months helping me relearn the basics from walking, talking and everything else in between. In the beginning, she would sit by my bedside and make a bargain with me. If I stayed with her for a little while longer, she would put another row on a crocheted blanket she was making for me.

Later, she would take my finger and make me count the stitches. One day she picked out a few skeins of yarn in varying shades of blue. She completed a few stitches before passing the crochet hook and yarn to me.

I know it hurts to be here, but I want you to stay with me, please. Just for a little while, okay? Count the stitches with me baby. Just try. Please?

The blanket the two of us made was lost between moves from one place to another. To this day, crochet has been my constant. There is a wall in my office filled with shelves upon shelves of yarn. Even though our stitches were different, her peach-scented hand cream was always there. And it didn't matter how threadbare the thing had gotten over the years. All I remember was her placing my fingers on the stitches and her faith in the God she served. I remember her taking those skeins and bridging the gap between us. I remember her building a bridge out of lace in the air to lead me back to her.

Most, if not all, of the prayer shawls, blankets, hats, and other bits and bobs I donate to charities across the country. Some even make it into the hands of my friends and family. I've had family members tell me that when they see me crocheting, they think of my mother. All I can do is smile.

I think of her too.

The Edge of Goodbye

My mother was one of the strongest people I know. There is a picture of her in dress whites—nurse's uniform—on my refrigerator. I pass it each day and whisper "Good Morning". I think about her smile and her tissue paper soft hands. I remember her singing off key to one of her favorite rock bands.

"I will put another row on your blanket if you stay with me, Stephanie. For every second that you stay, I'll put another row... I know it hurts and maybe you don't want to. You were meant to be here, Stephanie. You are going to touch so many lives, but you have to stay here. Not for me, but for you."

People talk about their heroes and idols. When I think of those words, I think of my mom. For every victory and every defeat, I always want her. Initially: My aunt's discouraging words nearly stopped my writing, but remembering my mother helped me overcome it. When whispers of a book deal came to me, I wanted my mother. When it dragged on with no answer one way or another, I wanted her. When other book deals came and went because I told the truth, I wanted my mother. When all I wanted was some place clean and quiet…it is always my mother that I want. Not friends or family or a celebratory drink. It is and will always be her that I want.

"You were a living doll when I brought you home for the second time. I had to teach you how to walk and talk again. You had to relearn so much and look at you now. You'll do the things I never got a chance to do. You'll travel and you'll cry, but you'll keep moving ... living."

I remember the day my mother died as clearly as the day I spoke my first words, "The bacon is burning." She'd been sick for a while but seemed to be coming out of it. I went to fix her breakfast that morning in October. The air had that bite to it that I came to call 'a rumor of snow'. We had already spent half the morning reminiscing about the works of AA Milne and how his adventures of a bear and his boy was the inspiration for my first nickname courtesy of that stuffed 'silly old bear'.

"The day you graduated from high school I searched everywhere for that mangy old teddy bear you clung to. I wanted to clean him up and stitch any threadbare places, because he'd been there when I couldn't be. But then you held him up as you crossed the stage."

The day she left this earth; I'd returned to making my mother's breakfast and gathered her medication that morning. I went back to ask her if she wanted me to freshen up her cup of coffee. At first, I thought she was sleeping or praying.

My mother's salt and pepper gray hair always felt like wavy cornsilk under my fingers. I brushed it back from her face and she sandwiched my hand between hers and smiled.

"You had every right to hate the world," she said. "I hated it for you."

I settled on the side of the bed and smiled. Years later, we rarely talked about my gang rape or the years of rehabilitation that followed. But the memories were close and when they overwhelmed her, she'd squeeze my hand and say, "They didn't know my girl."

The natural order of things dictates that a parent dies before their child. When that parent is your world and one of the main reasons why you are still in it, do the same rules apply? Of the many lessons my mother taught me, there was one she left out.

She never taught me how to say goodbye.

My mother pulled me close and embraced me for a long time. She pressed her nose into my hair like always and breathed me in deep. "Promise me something," she said releasing me.

"Anything," I replied trying to swallow past the lump in my throat.

"Write your stories, Stephanie. Write a bunch of them. Scary ones. Funny ones. Throw in a sad one too. Mix them up but write them." She released me and reached for the slips of paper spread out on the crochet blanket she made for me. The light and dark blue chevrons had faded some, but the love she crocheted there, the promises she stitched there still rang true.

She pressed the pages into my hand. "It's good Steph, really good. Write your stories your way with your words. Promise me."

I embraced her once more and moved to stand and she clung to me. "Promise me."

"I promise, Mom. I promise."

I felt her nod as she buried her face in the warm space between my neck and shoulder. She nodded and pressed a kiss to my shoulder before letting me go.

"I'll make you a fresh cup of coffee," I said, peering in her cup. "You barely touched this one."

"Okay," she chirped before picking up a few loose pages from my manuscript. "I have a couple more pages to finish. By the time you come back, I'll be done, and we can talk about it."

I hurried away with her mug of stale coffee in one hand and the pages I had written in longhand tucked under an arm. I took my time arranging her plate and morning meds on her napkin. Her orange juice glass was half full, just the way she liked it, with three ice cubes floating in that liquid sunshine. Fresh coffee filled her black wide-mouth mug and scrambled eggs with cheese over-flowed her plate. For once, I hadn't burned the bacon. I cut her toast into triangles, as preferred. We were going to sit and talk about my book and read from classics with soft strains of

Beethoven playing through the house because it was Sunday. And everybody knows. Sundays were for reading.

My Mom looked like she was sleeping or praying. The last pages still lay neatly stacked on her lap. By the time the ambulance arrived, I already had her on the floor performing CPR. When the paramedic put a hand on my shoulder, I knew. My mother's last breaths in this world came from me and they weren't enough.

I couldn't save the woman that saved me.

The Albatross

My brother locked himself in his bedroom with a sawed-off shotgun. Survivor's guilt plagued my brother and losing our mother made living a preposterous thing for a man as big as a bear with a laugh to match. Over the years, there would be many attempts and medications he would consume to keep the voices and the memories at bay.

I can only imagine what he felt knowing his friend had betrayed him. The one and only time we spoke about it, Lucas gave me the strangest look. The mixture of anguish and rage on his face made me back away.

People kept asking me how could I not know? I didn't. I really didn't. I mean, he helped me look for you. Helped me make signs and post them. Sat at the hospital with me. Cried with me.

I caught him once and beat the living shit out of him. He begged me to kill him. I decided not to. I wanted him to live with what he'd done every day of his life. He ended up in prison. From what I hear he got a taste of what you went through. When he killed himself, I thought I would be happy. I wasn't. Didn't take away what was done, and it didn't make me feel any better.

Lucas closed himself up in his room with that weapon he requested from one of my mother's boyfriends. Where my mother's request that I stay encouraged me, when I asked Lucas to stay, the words fell short. The idea that his so-called friends had helped him search for me hung like an albatross around his neck.

I never blamed my brother for what happened to me. I felt like he lost his innocence right along with me. Lucas trusted them, played video games and touch football with them. They betrayed him. I knew there weren't enough tears in me, but to see that effect on my brother who was larger than life, made the spider cracks in my world spread.

If I was late returning from school, then I was dead in a dumpster. If I went to the bathroom and stayed too long, he was afraid that I had finally had enough of the world and went to join our mother. Cancer and mental illness were the twin sins that plagued our family. Cancer seemed to have a particular interest in the women and the men walked a fine line between brilliance and madness. Lucas was cursed with both by the end.

I stood at his bedroom door flanked by police officers willing to break down the door to end his one-person standoff one way or another. After her funeral, my brother confided in me that suicide by cop would have suited him just fine.

When you came home, you needed Mom. She never blamed me, not even once. Even though I wanted her to. Mom never... something has to end the pain so that I can sleep. I don't think I've slept a night through since you came home. When I die, you're gonna be all alone just like before. At least I won't have to see it.

As we dismantled my mother's library and prepared to move, I found one of my mother's textbooks. Within the pages in her fine swirling scrawl, she left a note for me. I like to think she planned to give the book to me for a birthday or Christmas.

"Do the things I never got a chance to do. Write your stories. Write them your way with your words."

Her inscription was the only comfort I had when they were both gone.

My Funny Valentine/ Operation Uplift Stephanie

. . .

ALL OF THAT paled in comparison to February 16, 2021.

The holidays came and went, and the new year came in. February loomed in the not-too-distant future. Every year, the depression would crowd in, and the memories would wash over me. The nightmares never faded, but they came more frequently in grisly detail during that one month. Most mornings found me huddled in the corner forever watching the front door or soaking in a bath of bleach to try and scrub away the shame.

Little did I know, Naleighna had devised a plan. She spoke with members of the tribe about changing the narrative about three days in February. Without telling them anything about my unspeakable, she asked members of her tribe .... *Our* tribe to reach out to me by phone, by text or messenger with prayers, encouragement, and funny memes. She set up a schedule for something called *My Funny Valentine*.

Tribe came through.

People who were strangers to me a few months before flocked to Naleighna's side and signed up for a time slot on that schedule. They took time out of their day, their lives, to pour love and light into me. With a phone call or a text, they all stepped into my darkness and swathed my mental and spiritual wounds in love and light.

When we spoke that morning during the time she scheduled for herself, the words seemed to swell in my throat, but I managed to say them

You remembered.

That year, Naleighna and the tribe gave me a list of comedies to watch and the promise that the following year, I would celebrate the day after February 16th as the day I survived.

February 2022 came with bitter snow and nightmares that made smiling a chore. A knock at my door changed all of that. Naleighna had told me she wanted to celebrate her birthday on

February fourth with me over Zoom. I assumed we would sit on a video call and share some laughs while we ate whatever food she would have delivered.

But there was a knock at my door and a cryptic message sent via text … *Food be coming.*

When I swung the door open, nothing could have prepared me for what I saw. At first, I thought my eyes were deceiving me. A woman with sister locs, light brown complexion, and a wide smile was at my front door having flown out of a blizzard in Chicago to spend the weekend of her birthday with me.

But she wasn't alone. Dr. Vanessa Howard traveled by plane and Pastor Patty Harris by car to come and see me. All I could do was sob. I sat across the table from them at Mission Barbecue, shocked by what they had done for me. The next day, Florenza Denise Lee arrived after her flight had been canceled the day before because of another blizzard in her home state. There I was thinking we were going to pick up lost baggage and instead my sister soul mate, as she calls me, was there.

We had dinner at a local Indian restaurant and Zoomed with our Operation Uplift Stephanie team. The following day, we had breakfast at Roost and then went to a Pennsylvania Dutch Market to shop for crystals.

Over that weekend, each of my soul sisters took me aside and spoke words of wisdom into my life. They reminded me that beyond all shadows of a doubt. I wasn't alone anymore and then they proved it. Naleighna informed me that not only was the small circle of women there with me in on the weekend, but the entire tribe was in on it months prior to their arrival.

Tribe flooded my mailbox with letters and cards and gifts that not only covered my desk, but also decorated my soul. Through my panic attacks and my tears, the tribe… my tribes Namakir, Nakaeri, and Namapro flooded my life with love and laughter and light. The event included a comedy show, drawing a larger crowd with the addition of Staci Wilson, Kadesha Powell, Christine

Pauls, Terrie Ann Johnson, Royce Slade Morton, and Bunny Ervin.

Each day and every evening was filled with something that they all planned down to the last detail. One night, Naleighna, Pastor Patty, and Dr. Vanessa Howard sat on the floor and taught me to play a card game called Spoons, like little children. The laughter, my God, the laughter was like music or living water flowing over the cursed, parched soil of my soul.

I don't remember eating anything wherever we went. I was too busy looking around the tables at my tribe, my family that cared enough to travel from all corners to celebrate Naleighna and Staci's birthday and break bread with me. A band of angels, each extending a wing built a hedge around me. They gave me a fresh memory for when the landscape changes and the night grows teeth in February.

They prayed with me. Naleighna and Vanessa sang for me. Pastor Patty prayed for me. And then there was Florenza looping her arm around mine, pulling me back from the brink when the panic attacks made breathing impossible. Her practical but hilarious observation had me laughing through my tears.

The more you cry, the less you pee.

They cried with me and as we stood in a circle on that last day in their hotel room; I felt something break within me. It felt much like the scratchy smock I imagined Susanna, who I wrote about in my memoir, *Survivor*, wore in the prison. It fell from my body.

No words adequately explain what they did for me that weekend. *Operation Uplift Stephanie* made being here hurt a little less. No, a *lot* less.

Next year, I won't be celebrating the pain as I have done for far too long. I will not commune with the shame and guilt that was never mine to begin with. Next year, and for every year to follow, I celebrate the day after my unspeakable.

I honor the day I survived.

SURVIVING GENERATIONAL
TRAUMA BY NALEIGHNA KAI

"*What would I know about being enough when I was reduced to the lowest common denominator the day I was born?* – Naleighna Kai

What had happened was . . . I was adopted by my biological mother. Yes, you read that right. On the day I was born, my mother signed herself into Cook County Hospital as her sister, Rose. Then, she pushed until I emerged from her body, dropped me into my aunt's arms, left the hospital, and didn't look back. Until fate gave her no other choice.

My "new" mother/aunt raised me for eighteen months, then made a disastrous mistake that earned her a trip to prison. What a family, right?

Unfortunately, I landed back in the one place my biological mother never wanted me to be—her home. To make matters worse, while my brother and sister were babysitting me, I swallowed some type of household cleaner. I ended up with a medical emergency which put me in the hospital for weeks. My biological mother was forced to go before the judge and tell the truth about what she'd done when I was first born. The result? I was adopted by my biological mother.

Here is where things became more interesting. When I first arrived at that three-bedroom apartment in the Robert Taylor Homes, a project on the South Side of Chicago, I went directly to my mother's friend—a woman I had never laid eyes on before. I crawled into her lap and went to sleep. That woman, Sandy, became someone I call my "true mother".

My biological mother had been through a great deal herself, and later on, the manner of my conception came to light. My father forced my mother—this added insult to life's already plentiful set of injuries. Before I was born, she had taken three drastic measures to make sure I never saw the light of day. Hangers. Throwing herself down the stairs and other ways of physically harming herself. Large doses of quinine sulfate. This isn't something I'm guessing about. This is something she told me.

So, imagine how bitter and angry she was at having to raise the very child she wanted nothing to do with. When I was born, she had taken another path—giving me to someone who would actually love me.

Evidently, there were some life lessons for us to learn, because I was back under her roof and the physical and emotional abuse I endured was substantial. The only person who tried to protect me was my true mother, who stayed in an emotionally abusive friendship far longer than she should have; all because she felt the need to be there for me.

At age fourteen, I was curvaceous and built like the proverbial brick s*%thouse which attracted the wrong kind of male attention —*Adult* male attention.

Aunt-mother Rose had served her prison sentence and was back in Chicago. I ran away to live with her—the woman who raised me for the initial eighteen months of my life.

One night, I overheard Aunt Rose making arrangements for her brother—my uncle—to visit every week to have sex with me. I was fourteen and realized my safety was not a given, even around her. Trust me, I didn't stick around to find out the end result of that. Instead, I fled to the supposed safety of my father's home.

My mother had not told anyone of what my father had done to her, so I didn't realize living with him wouldn't make me any safer than being with her or my aunt. He would show up to our house in a uniform, bearing gifts, and a bag of silver dollars as well. I saw him as a sort of Santa Claus. I didn't realize why my mother was so cold and distant, but I was happy to see him because I didn't know anything better.

I'll state this simply: my father didn't respect my right to say no, and I endured two months of pure hell. The ordeal happened during the summer, when no school officials or teachers would come looking for me because there was no place I was "supposed" to be. No one knew I was "missing". No one knew I had run to him. No one knew I was in danger.

My father made the fortunate mistake of untying me from the portable cot that was my existence for several weeks at a time. While he was escorting me on an infrequent trip to the bathroom, somehow I had enough strength left to bolt for the window, prepared to die so I could finally put an end to that nightmare.

Breaking through the glass, instead of crashing into a crumpled, bloody mess on the concrete, I actually landed on my feet. The shock of that effort ripped through me. As traffic passed by on Michigan Avenue, I stood there, amazed at coming through in one piece. No broken bones, only small cuts here and there. Totally naked. Starved and undernourished, much thinner than when I arrived two months prior, and probably looking a frightful mess.

Two women having a smoke on the porch quickly gathered me up. They ushered me inside their apartment before my father could get dressed and make it down the stairs. They were going to call the police, but I stopped them. My father carried two holstered guns and some type of badge. I wasn't sure what agency he worked for, but he was great friends with several police officers in that area. Police would not be of any help. So I asked the women to call the one person who I never thought would be in my life again.

My biological mother.

While sitting in the back of my brother's navy-blue Chevy Caprice, wearing clothes that the women had given me after they bathed me, my bio mother tried to get me to talk about what happened. I didn't talk. I didn't speak. I was numb, tired, and still afraid that even she wouldn't be able to protect me from him. Besides, she had already done enough damage to me on her own. I didn't trust her either. She had a mean streak a mile long. From the time that she would beat me with extension cords then force me into a bath of scalding water; to another time when she beat me so bad that my eyes shut and I couldn't go to school for a week. Or when she gleefully proclaimed that she would put me on punishment for six months out of a year to cover Christmas, my birthday, and Easter and so she didn't have to buy me anything. Oh, let's not forget the time the church had a trip to Disney World and I had to stay in the hotel the entire week and never got to see the place.

When she picked me up from those women who rescued me, my mother twisted the knife my father's abuse had anchored in my back by saying, "Whatever happened to you was good for you."

Yes, she actually said that without knowing what he'd done. Only later when writing the novel, *She Touched My Soul*, did I understand that she probably *did* know, because he'd done the same thing to her. But with just those few words, her need to always be right and to punish me for embarrassing her by running away, returned me to the natural order of things. Yes, I was home. Back to the norm of emotional assault, and physical abuse that I could actually welcome after being held hostage in one of my father's many apartments.

Thankfully, my true mother returned the moment she found out I was back at the house on Merrion Avenue. She had left the moment I went to stay with Aunt-Mother Rose. My mother wasn't all that kind to her either. My true mother, Sandy, was the one who helped me at the beginning stages of healing; trying to make sure that I didn't shut myself off from the world.

Unfortunately, it would be years before the real healing took place.

All I had to do was make it four more year, then none of my childhood experiences would matter, right?

A few years after I escaped from my father's clutches, my mother and I were in a rebellion fueled tug-of-war. One evening, she fixed butter beans for dinner. I did not like them, Sam I am, and would not eat them with green eggs and ham. My mother was insulted and said that if I didn't eat them, I couldn't eat anything else in her house.

Well, that was fine by me. The lunchroom ladies at school would feed me. That worked, until my mother's spies snitched. When she figured out she wasn't winning this particular battle, she moved the goal post by saying, "If you don't eat at home, you can't eat anywhere else."

So, for a month I was on water only, and even though I wasn't eating, I was throwing up, so I thought I was sick. I only took a pregnancy test because my cycle had stopped.

During that time, my sister, Eve was also pregnant. The horrible encounters with Eve led to me staying locked in my room, the sharpest knives in the house in hand, while she placed a few calls to the police.

While I was listening in on another extension, one of the dispatch women asked my sister "Honey, where is y'all's mother?"

My sister replied, "She's in California."

The dispatcher shot back, "If I had raised two fools, I'd be in California, too."

That night, I was in such pain, and my sister just watched as I crawled down the stairs to get help. She didn't lift a finger. The ambulance took me to the nearest hospital, but I lost the baby along the way. So the day I found out I was pregnant was the same day I miscarried. I will forever remember the kindness and compassion of those two emergency personnel. One said, "Honey, you're only seventeen. You have a lot of life ahead."

Considering what I had been through early in life, I didn't think there was a maternal bone in my body. So what happened to me at age eighteen? Right at the point where I didn't know my worth and I was about to put a "for sale" sign on one thigh and an "open for business" sign on the other? You guessed it, that star in the east floated by, along with Three Wise Men. In either case, I was now expecting the one thing I never believed I could handle. How was I going to raise a child—a *man* child—without infecting him with the aftermath of my traumatic experiences? Why would The Creator put me in such a predicament? Were they passing the peace pipe up there in Heaven?

I didn't set out to get pregnant at seventeen by a twenty-five-year-old man, but we also didn't consistently do what it took for me not to get pregnant either. Should've known something was off about the man when he asked me out on a date while I was sitting between my mother's thighs with a half head full of hair relaxer. Who does that?

A year after my miscarriage, I was pregnant again. I did not want to be, and my body was doing all it could to accommodate me. My son almost didn't make it here. The first two months, I was deathly ill. Couldn't keep water down. Was bringing stuff back up that didn't look anything like what I'd eaten. Three months into turning eighteen, in college, still living at home, and pregnant.

Dr. Gervais eventually decided to take the baby, or else both of us might die. On the night before I was scheduled for the procedure, I had a dream that changed my entire life. Isn't it strange that in the beginning of my life my mother didn't want me? And now I felt the same. I didn't believe I would be a good person to raise anyone. The dream reassured me that everything would be all right.

When I woke, it was time for me to go to the hospital. I didn't. For the first time in a while I had a full meal. And it wasn't a lightweight breakfast kind of thing either. Leftovers of Salisbury steak, mashed potatoes and gravy, mixed vegetables with lots of corn, and fresh biscuits, and some Kool-Aid. Yes, red—the *best* kind! This stayed down, and so did every meal thereafter.

The difference was that I wanted my child and now my body was trying to accommodate.

Michael Reese Hospital in Chicago was a teaching hospital. I didn't quite understand what that meant, and was none too pleased when a crew of doctors came in and all of them started checking out "the goods."

I told the doctor, "You know, I'm going to start charging admission."

He tilted his head then responded, "But we're only hanging out in the lobby."

"Yes, but the view of the movie is still the same," I replied and held out my hand. "So pay up."

They laughed so hard that they couldn't do anything else for a few moments before he ushered all of them out of the room.

My first experience with unconditional love was a tiny, unexpected bundle of joy. He took a little longer than expected to get here. My son fell asleep while I was in labor. The nurses had to come in and shake my stomach from time to time. Shoot, if he knew what I knew about what was waiting on the outside, he would've stayed inside.

Jeremy finally arrived, and he was absolutely beautiful. Actually, I'm exaggerating, because he looked like he'd been through the wringer. He had ivory skin, purple lips, and slanted eyes, which made me swear up and down they were passing off someone else's child. Maybe they needed to place him back in the oven and put him on broil for a few more minutes. Thankfully, he soon fleshed out and became a beautiful little bundle of joy. And that's the truth. During those twenty-six hours of labor, I read three novels, plus eight Harlequin romances, and took notes on everything. I kept a journal from pregnancy to delivery, writing in it regularly until he was six, then turning it over to him to continue.

Motherhood was especially rewarding. Here was someone who depended on me for everything. A little person who seemed to live for my smiles, my hugs, and my voice. A person who needed my protection. A person who I would keep safe at all costs. A person who would inspire me to take risks I would not have dared on my own.

My mother was partial to boys and spoiled them rotten. That was not how I wanted my son to grow up. Even at nineteen, I felt that the best thing I could do as a parent was make sure he was a good person, able to take care of himself, live out his life's desires, and achieve more than I ever had. That could never happen under her roof. I never wanted him to experience any of the sexual abuse that I had, nor did I want him to be spoiled, lazy, and unable to take responsibility for his actions or his life.

When my son was six months old, I was still reeling from the blows life had whopped upside my head and other places. What I had was such a strong desire to have my own home that it manifested in a miraculous way. And it came from *acting as if* I already had the space. I purchased new dishes, bed linen, silverware, and glasses, and hid them under my son's crib in the tiny room that I slept in.

The neighbors I stayed with from time to time because my mother and I weren't getting along, were losing their home. The father was a veteran. When they moved out of the property to allow the foreclosure process to move forward, they allowed me to slide in and changed the utilities into my name.

At the time, my only source of income was public assistance, definitely not enough to truly live on, but it kept us afloat until the Veteran's Administration came calling. They found that I was maintaining the premises, and gave me the opportunity to purchase the home. I landed a position with the City of Chicago, and combined with Avon sales, and a crew of high school students selling chocolate fundraiser candy bars all helped me come up with the down payment and to qualify for the house. The man who worked for the V.A. gave me grace, and The Creator showed me favor.

All I knew was that I wanted a house, and this one was three doors down from my mother. The perfect starter home—three bedrooms, one bath, kitchen, living room, and a basement. Trust me, I didn't know anything about the regular progression of life—apartment, *then* a house. I wasn't taught any of that. Nothing about saving, building credit, or anything. My mother and her best friend were masters of something that was called "kiting". They would float checks back and forth into their bank accounts to help each other pay bills. A lot of people did that back in the day. That was when clearing houses took a few days to actually process "checks". They certainly couldn't get away with doing that these days. And for some reason my brother trusted her with his money. He'd deposit his paychecks into her account and she was supposed to pay his bills. Well in all of her finagling she missed a car payment. Or two. Or three. And because she wasn't listed on his account she couldn't call in and make arrangements. She was afraid to tell him, so he was truly surprised when he walked out one morning to go to work and his car was gone.

That's the kind of financial blueprint she gave me—being a passenger on the struggle bus. At nineteen, I now had my own home and could raise my son my way. My mother was so angered that I wouldn't let her take over raising my son that she treated him differently. Her actions were obvious to everyone. Only later when he was about nine or so, did my son pick up on her attitude, and he was saddened by it. He loved his grandmother. Truly loved her. But she only saw him as an extension of me. She hated the fact that I desired for my son to turn out better than my brother and nephews—males she had raised.

Then something happened to my near perfect child. At the same time my son was having an out-of-body puberty experience,

I was having an episode of my own. Well, not the puberty part, but this wasn't the best time for either of us. My reaction to what was going on with him made me look even deeper at myself, which put me on the initial path of healing. I finally told someone what my father had done. I was twenty-six.

My son was in his own world of pain, wondering what was so wrong with him—a karate, football, and baseball champ, an honor student—that his father didn't love him.

Me? I was wondering what was so wrong with me that The Creator would start my life by giving me a ringside seat by the fire, next to Satan himself.

Writing My Way to Healing

Fast forward to December 1999. I finally was able to write about my traumatic experiences, weaving them into a fictional format. Soon after publishing *She Touched My Soul*, I started receiving emails from women who had been through similar circumstances.

This is how I found my purpose—healing. Overcoming pain, obstacles, and challenges. I didn't know a novel could help with that. Some women will probably never seek help. I didn't. The kind of help I needed found me! My boss at the social services agency where I worked, heard my story and eventually became my sexual abuse counselor. She later became my pastor, and even more importantly, one of my best friends. She came into my life when the timing was exactly right. I was ready to heal.

My father was taken to the hospital two days later with blood poisoning. No, it wasn't my true mother's handiwork or mine. But that timing, though? If I had told her back when it first happened at age fourteen, she would've killed him. But I was well aware that I needed her more than justice needed to be served.

Being his only known living relative, I spent two months going back and forth miles away to Olympia Fields Hospital to handle his medical care. Finally, one day a friend of mine said, "He's waiting for you to forgive him."

In my heart, forgiveness was the last thing he deserved. But I had to give it some thought. My father's condition was such that he couldn't move a muscle, nor could he take in proper food sustenance. He couldn't even blink his lids across eyes that stayed open 24/7. Almost a mirror image of some of the things I experienced while living with him. The doctor let me know they needed to remove the skin from around his genitals because it was turning blue. I finally gave in, stood by his bedside and said, "Daddy, I forgive you."

When I made it home that day, the hospital had called and left a message. My father had passed away not long after I left his room.

Now for the reality of things. It took *years* for that statement of forgiveness to become a reality. Mostly because the real issue was that the person I truly needed to forgive was *myself*. Thoughts of *If only I had stayed and endured my biological mother's abuse", "If only I had the stomach for what my aunt was setting me up to do with my uncle," "If only—fill in the blank—... then none of this would have happened.*

Breaking the Cycle

Year after year, my son never ceased to amaze me. My son had such a wonderful disposition that people wanted to give him everything, because he asked for nothing. That smile, that voice, that face—that sweetness in his soul that did not reflect me or his father—endeared so many people to him. He was never materialistic and that made people do more for him than he realized. For his birthday, he wanted to have friends and family over—it was never about presents.

He also did not like to disappoint people. All I had to do was point out something that wasn't right, and he was instantly sorry for what he'd done wrong.

Overall, I thought, "Hey, this motherhood thing isn't so bad after all." I enrolled in adoption classes.

Then my son hit puberty and lost his entire mind on a more permanent basis.

Soon, the adoption people were calling me, saying, "You haven't been to classes lately." Frustrated as I was at the time, I replied, "Sweetheart, let me tell you something. I don't want this little m_____r I already have, and I don't want your little m_____rs either." Remember, I wasn't Little Miss Sunshine, so I'll let you fill in the blanks.

She asked my son's age. I said twelve, she laughed and asked me to call them back in a couple of years.

They're still waiting.

Sometimes I took discipline a step too far. Mirroring my mother when I swore up and down that would never happen. At one point, I ended up sending him to stay with his Godmother for a while. He had almost burned the house down with a gift of fireworks from his father that he hid in the hamper near the heating element in his bedroom! My son was so afraid of the punishment I might dole out that he ran out of the house, butt naked, no shoes, in the dead of winter, with six feet of snow on the ground.

He deserved to be disciplined—a rare occurrence of about once a year—but not with a severity that put such a primal fear in him. He did not deserve that.

Now, here's the interesting part. That period of my life was a rough time all around, and it probably had less to do with my son's actions—some of which were life-threatening, due to his father's intervention—than the fact that I had finally found the courage to tell my true mother what had happened to me during those two months I lived with my father the summer of my fourteenth year.

After my confession, as expected, she was ready to end his life.

Forgiveness

NOW HERE'S where I know I'm on the path to manifesting healthier relationships. My son was home from college and I thought he needed a little shaking up in order to get him on a more productive path. Part of the issue was a lesson in sweat equity—when you're not contributing as much to a household financially, you give it by doing more around the house. He was not feeling that. And I wasn't feeling the fact that he wasn't feeling that.

On my birthday I had to take out the garbage and do the dishes, I made a decision to have peace in my house. That was my present to myself. My action, in my mind, was *totally* correct. But the timing of it was all wrong. On the coldest day in Chicago in decades, when cars were frozen and stuck on Lake Shore Drive, I packed his things and had them waiting for him when he came home. I let him know he could take the suitcase right now or come back with a truck and get it all at once. I found out much later that he had walked forty blocks in the snow to a friend's house. Two months later he was in an apartment.

This was the first time we ever had a break in our relationship. Even still, I threw him a housewarming party.

Years later, he was in Costco and I called him with the video feature on and asked him to call me back when he had a moment. He said he did right then. I apologized to him for putting him out of the house that bitterly cold day so long ago. I confessed that while it was the right thing to do to shake him out of whatever funk he had fallen into, it was the absolute wrong time.

"I don't want to leave this earth without giving you the apology you deserve," I told him.

He said, "Come on, Mom. Don't have me crying in Costco." But he did shed a tear or two right then and there! Then, he who had gone to Fisk University, then South Carolina State, graduated from Columbia College, walked the red carpet when he was nominated for an NAACP Image Award, married the love of his life, said, "I forgave you for that a long time ago."

Two weeks later, a video call came while I was at home and he wanted to talk. Evidently, his beloved had a little "come to Jesus meeting with him". And it ended with him understanding exactly what I meant all those years ago, so he apologized to me. And I said, "Come on, son. Don't have me crying in Costco."

Those words are now an inside joke for us.

The apology I never received from the people that hurt me. How healing those words must have been for him.

He did write about his life experience in the book, *Super-woman's Child: Son of a Single Mother* and *Wisdom: Blessings From Imperfections*. Recounting the incident from his point of view didn't necessarily put me in the best light. He asked my permission before putting it in print. I told him that it was his story, his truth, and I would not censor him in any way. Writing was his way of healing, and parents reading it would definitely understand where I was coming from. When he was going off to his freshman year at Fisk University, I apologized to him for the first time. The second one came in Costco.

My mother wasn't taught to balance a checkbook, so she couldn't teach me. Therefore, I didn't teach my son. Which meant the cycle would continue if someone didn't embrace a different way of living. That someone had to be me.

Learning from my son

Sometimes the thing we think we don't want is the very thing we need for our spiritual development. We'll swear up and down that we'll never do X, Y, or Z. And The Creator says, "Oh, yeah? Let's see what we can do about that." Basically, it's because energy follows thought. When you put emphasis on what you *don't* want, it's taking the focus off the things you *do* want. And trust me, the things you don't want always come with a calling card—*remember that statement you made a kabillion years ago? Well, since you feel so strongly about it, you must really want to tackle it.* And then ... BAM! Suddenly you're paddling upstream without a boat or a paddle. You're now grappling with a challenge that you swore you never wanted to wade through in the first place.

The Creator knew to pair me up with the perfect child to facilitate a series of lessons of loving someone outside of myself. My relationship with my son also opened me to realizing there were more important things in life than the darkness I'd experienced growing up.

There's a Bible verse that says, *The blessing of the LORD, it maketh rich, and he addeth no sorrow with it.* Proverbs 10:22 And I also learned about the law of assumption, which is different from the law of attraction, which encourages the understanding that everyone is prosperous.

Armed with that knowledge, my thinking shifted. What I did was attract an understanding that struggle was not my birthright. What I did was attract the resources, books, and people who could teach me a better way. What I also did was attract the things I desired, which made me flex my faith muscles, which also came with an understanding that I had to put in the work. I could have faith all day long, but if it wasn't followed by intentions and actions, it would be nothing more than wishful thinking.

Only by shaking off that original birthright and pattern was I able to expand my consciousness and accept that I *could* be wealthy, which eventually transformed into I *should* be wealthy. And I'm not just talking about dollars and cents.

Buying my first house at nineteen years old was due to the determination to have a safe place to raise my son. My writing career began from my desire to heal.

My original limiting belief was that my life was supposed to be lived in pain. My original limiting belief was that I was supposed to experience lack and limitation. I was supposed to carry the weight for twenty-six years and it would take equally as long to overcome and heal. My original limiting belief was that I could only live paycheck to paycheck. My original limiting belief was that I had to struggle to make ends meet, before I met the end.

I am come that they might have life, and that they might have it more abundantly. John 10:10.

Final Notes:

Some women might not ever pick up the type of books that could point them toward counseling or something else that would help them to heal; such as *You Can Heal Your Life* or *Empowering Women* (both by Louise Hay). But some of them picked up *She Touched My Soul, Loving Me for Me, My Time in the Sun*, or *Was it Good For You Too?*—all novels penned by me—and they were helped in some way.

My writing also changed the people who were around me. And my life. My inner circle, is now filled with people who love me unconditionally.

Remember this: You were not put on this earth to struggle. You were put here to be victorious. And it starts with embracing that you could be—no, actually you are prosperous.

"When a flower doesn't bloom, you fix the environment in which it grows, not the flower."—Alexander Den Heijer

FAITH AND FORGIVENESS BY
RANDI COLEY

$\mathcal{M}$y mother's womb must have been a hostile work environment. Five of her seven children are mentally ill and receiving combat pay in the form of disability checks. I was one of "the normal ones", but that didn't make me immune to the malice that some of my siblings poured out on me like honey for the ants to feast on.

The horror level varies in survival stories, according to some. I don't subscribe to that point of view. Over the years and plenty of therapy sessions and prayer, I've come to understand that the twin sins of trauma and atrocity meet us where we are. The effects of both can last a lifetime as the memories become the invisible scars we wear, like Joseph's coat of many colors.

In situations like these, we wonder where God is and if the faith and forgiveness He speaks of even applies to our situations. For a time...a long time, I believed those gifts belonged in everyone else's pocket but mine. The verbal and sexual abuse I endured at the hands of my sister Thomasina, "Tommy" to her friends and family, served as my proof.... or so I thought.

One of the last confrontations I had with her was during a

routine visit. My daughter, parched from the day's journey, asked for a glass of water. My sister was deep in the weeds of cleaning her home.

"Why don't you take care of your bastard baby before you take them to someone's house? Why is she asking for something to drink?" Tommy snarled, before returning to her chores.

How a simple request for a glass of water escalated to a Battle Royale was beyond me, but typical of my sister. The fight happened on Mother's Day when children were supposed to be kinder to one another in honor of the woman that gave them life and taught them how to use a spoon. Apparently, my sister didn't get the memo. One of my other sisters requested I do a wellness check on Tommy.

It's the charitable... Godly thing to do.

That sister's nasally voice echoed in my ears every time she asked me to complete this maudlin task, hoping for a different outcome. The same words muttered under my breath just made me more and more apprehensive as I drove closer to my sister Tommy's house. I kept telling myself that this time had to be different. It just had to be. We were adults now, with lives of our own. Surely we could do better...be better. As I looked at the deteriorating driving conditions that surrounded me, the answer was obvious. A major rainstorm left treacherously flooded areas in its wake and forced me to park a couple of blocks away. Looking back, I realize that this was a red flag. I mean, why should I be risking the safety of myself and my five-year-old daughter for a sister that seemed to hate the air I breathed? Hindsight hammered home the point that I lacked boundaries, and the word "no" was a myth. No one heard me when I said it, anyway. But there I was, being the dutiful sister. I waded through the water with my daughter on my hip because it was the right thing to do. Right? Right?

My daughter's bottom lip quivered as tears welled in her eyes. Her tiny chest shook as an apology formed on her lips. I didn't have to guess at the shards of questions floating around in her mind.

Had she spoken out of turn? Had she done something wrong?

My child's unspoken questions mirrored my own constant worries.

"What is wrong with you? She's five. She asked for water, not the keys to your bleached clean kingdom," I said, waggling a finger.

When Tommy turned, the venom in her eyes spoke of bloody noses and infected scratches that leaked for days. My sister was almost always ready for a fight.

"You, young trifling Bastard all you ever do is have babies you can't take care of. Then you have the audacity to take them around other people, expecting someone to take up your slack. Why haven't you fed her? You have the nerve to come to *my* house with that baby that you insisted on having. How dare you stand there and act like everything is okay? I did not invite you and I sure don't want you here," she snapped while pointing in my child's general direction with the broom handle.

The unjust accusation made my baby cry. I should have known better than to bring her, but with no babysitter, I had no choice. It didn't change the simple truth that I knew what my sister was like.

All the signs were there whenever Tommy and I were in the same room. My older sister, the one that was supposed to love and protect me, was ready to put her hands on me or my daughter, and I was not about to let that happen. One of my other sisters, the one I called Polly Peacemaker, was trying to smooth things over, and that just made it worse.

I gathered my daughter into my arms. Her tiny body trembled against mine as I reached the door. I figured this particular storm would end if I removed myself from the situation. My mother used to tell us it was hard to have an argument in a room by yourself. Sounded good and the philosophy worked most times, but then I looked over my shoulder.

Tommy was taking the steps by two, charging at me with the broom in her hand. Making it out the door was no longer an option. I put my daughter down and ran up the stairs to face my sister. One minute we're fighting and the next her husband was pulling us apart like wayward school girls.

"What happened?" he asked, while wiping the sweat from his brow.

She pointed at me. "Get her out of here before I get my gun."

"What have I ever done to you?" I asked, "All I ever tried to do was love you."

Her blistering gaze cut across the miles of memory that separated us. "And somehow sleeping with my husband and having a baby is all about the sisterly bond? That filthy thing in your arms is proof of your lying, cheating ways! What a low-down dirty thing to do to your own blood," she spat. "You're gonna do a slow burn in hell, just like I always said."

Only then did my child's screaming snatch me back to reality. She cowered in the corner with her arms clasped over her head, as if to ward off the blows I received. I rushed down to gather her in my arms and just as I turned to go, Tommy spat at my back.

I turned on her so quickly that she stumbled backward. When she tried to advance again, her husband hooked an arm around her waist.

"Consider this, Tommy: If I was low down enough to sleep with your husband and have his child, do you really think I would work two jobs to make ends meet? Why settle for being some woman on the side when I could have the man? Isn't that right, Roger?"

When she came at me again, her husband grabbed her. "Enough Tommy! Just let her leave and stop all this foolishness. As for you," he said, glancing at the beautiful little girl in my arms with my eyes, nose, and chin, "You were asking for it like all y'all young girls do. I keep telling y'all I don't remember, I was high! I didn't know what I was doing. All you had to do was stay away from me."

I tilted my head like I hadn't heard him. "Kinda hard to do

when you ambushed me. Harder to scream with a hand clamped over your mouth and your heavy sweaty body pinning me to the bed. I was sixteen. What you did wasn't sex. It was sexual assault, plain and simple. Should I tell her what you whispered in my ear before you finished?"

"State could have locked him away," Tommy said. "We could have lost our home. He could have lost his job. All you had to do was keep your mouth shut. He already apologized."

"What about the other women, those you know he "cheated on you with." Or the possible other children running around out there that look so much like him? Was he high then? I counted at least two that he couldn't deny even if he tried. Strange how no matter how hard you tried; your womb and arms remain empty."

Roger swept his wife behind him, pinning her shoulder against the wall. "Shut up about that. No one disrespects my wife in our house! Don't you ever come back here, or maybe I *will* let my wife get her gun."

Part Two

HATING me was Tommy's religion.

It didn't matter if we spent all of Sunday at church, attended prayer meetings on Wednesdays and Vacation Bible School in the summer. Jesus was all about love. He taught it, lived it and showed it even on the day he died. My mother tried to instill the same in us, but where Tommy excelled in quoting scripture chapter and verse, The Word wasn't in her.

Why would it be?

When I left my sister's house for what I assumed was the last time, I shut down. Maybe I was all the horrific things my sister said I was.

Turn the other cheek. One of you has to be the bigger person. Family forgives. That's your sister!

Everyone seemed to have an opinion about the estranged relationship my sister and I had over the years. To this day, I always wondered about the surrounding people with their arsenal of platitudes and tone deaf advice. Was I that good at concealing the family secrets? *What happens here stays here.* Were they just that blind? Maybe they just didn't care. You know the phrase go along to get along? Maybe that was the best advice, because airing the family's dirty laundry was out.

Tommy was my inner voice and my first abuser. She took a perverse glee in my misery. My first memory of being molested by her, eclipsed everything. She told me I was dirty and spent hours making me feel that way. Her beatings were legendary, if not informative. She was the reason I learned the word *bastard.* She called me one. I didn't know what the word meant, so I looked it up. Depending on the context, I was either a despicable person or a child born out of wedlock. Anatomy and morality lessons aside. I am a twin, but for some unknown reason, I am the one she blamed for the destruction of her family when my mother filed for divorce from her father.

Dealing with her was a battle of wills. I was the butt of her jokes, and a pincushion for her rage. For years, my sister made it clear that my very existence was an affront to something deep within her that all but required that she pour out her malice on me without measure. I was everything but the name my mother gave me. I explained away the evidence of my beatings with some sad, strange accident that always befell me because I was clumsy.

Growing up, I felt like a mess of injuries and my sister's insults. Any talent or success I had with anything was a fluke or something to be ashamed of.

If Tommy was nothing else, she was thorough. She was convincing on a level of a veteran narcissist. Charismatic and a friend to all in public, but something entirely different behind closed doors. Watching me clean up blood after one of her remedial lessons became her favorite pastime. With my twin, and other siblings looking on or turning a blind eye to keep that illusion of peace, I accepted my plight. We all have a role to play in this life. I learned to toe the line. After all, she was the older sister, and I was The Bastard, the despicable one. I learned to measure the quality of my day based on Tommy's mood. I learned that behind every smile lurked a fist or a new fresh hell for some real or imagined slight, and it was always...always my fault.

I carried that foul philosophy into my adulthood. Apologies were my first defense. I watched for facial reactions and learned body language. People pleasing became instinct and boundaries. Boundaries were myths. I did what I was told and laughed off insults and any verbal or physical abuse directed my way because surely I deserved it. Obviously, I had done something to anger the person. Smiles were easy because I tried my hardest not to be a threat. Crying later in the darkness of my bedroom or in the shower became my canned response. I worked on forgiving Tommy and I tried to be kind whenever we crossed paths. I failed. And, as the years went by, those altercations happened less and less, until I avoided seeing her at all; another knee jerk reaction, but it was as good as any, I supposed.

Setting and keeping boundaries saved me over the years. Every time I dismissed them, I paid, sometimes in heartbreak or lost money or opportunities.

When I left my sister's home that Mother's Day, I took to my bed. It wasn't the first time I had had depression, but this round was so severe that it actually hurt to be here. It's funny and tragically strange how people think depression is a choice or a sadness that can be washed away or gotten over with a positive affirmation or two. I felt like I had been buried alive.

After six months, my closest friend convinced me to seek a counselor. It took a while to warm up to them, but when I did, little by little, the soil shifted and, like a flower, I slowly emerged. I worked on building better coping mechanisms and communication skills. I cultivated habits that would become part of my survival manual.

I established boundaries and learned a simple yet profound truth. I *mattered*. No longer did I have to view myself through the skewered optics my sister used. I did not base my self-worth on anyone else's opinion of me. My value didn't diminish when it was carried on breath soured by mental illness, jealousy, envy, or hatred. I determined my worth, and like a treasure or precious gift, I pocketed it for home and shared it with my children. I took the shards of my life and fused them together to make a valiant attempt at making my children whole.

When talking about boundaries, one thing that you have to start and know about yourself as an individual is where your boundaries lie. People often will set a boundary, but it doesn't become defined until they *enforce* it. Quite often, I discovered that when I set a boundary; I was accused of acting funny or thinking I was better than everyone else. Yes, I was better. Better than the old version of me that functioned with a lack of boundaries to keep the peace. It's funny how my lack of boundaries protected everyone's peace but my own. With that in mind, I changed the narrative. Was it easy, no. Was it necessary? Desperately so.

I wasn't the butt of my sister's jokes or something to be beaten into submission or dismissed altogether. I was a person with feelings, hopes, and dreams, and I deserved better. Learning this lesson took time. Family and friends still tested me. I was a wallet, or the little sister cast aside or mocked because I forgot the pecking order and my place in it. For them, it was all love because they told me so and I believed them.

Romantic relationships became casualties of my boundaries. There was even a time when my ex and I thought we could salvage a friendship, or so I thought. I loosened the rules because things were going smoothly, but he exploited that. There's truth in the adage that you teach people how to treat you. It took years to learn that particular lesson because it truly doesn't matter what you say. It's all about what you *do*.

Part Three

THEY TOLD me that time heals all wounds. For me, time and its twin—distance—tore open my scars and made them howl.

Avoidance became my drug of choice. Why step into the fray of a difficult relationship or situation when procrastination and evasion served as a sufficient Band Aid for an emotional gunshot wound?

For years, I refused to speak to Tommy. What was the point? Every time we were in the same room, an argument spawned like a school of piranhas. All it would take was a snide remark and our age old battle would begin again. I cannot tell you how many family functions were missed or ruined because of us.

Communication, or more to the point, my lack of skill in the art form became a sword I swung like a baseball bat. I had tools from therapy and my faith, but I didn't use them.

Something had to give.

Bitterness, unforgiveness, and rage...horrible rage colored everything I did. It was only later in the quiet that I realized I was flailing around in an ocean of grief. Grief for the child I should have been. Grieving...aching for answers, as I longed for peace. I secretly hoped to reconnect with my sister, even after all we'd been through.

Forgiveness sets you free if you allow it to.

My mother's long suffering, unending love for us all made sense. Even the scriptures I studied made it clear what I was supposed to do, but how? Any uneasy peace I had with my sister always reminded me of a time bomb ticking away. Eventually, we would be at each other's throats again. Why bother?

On some level, I felt entitled to my rage, but then it changed, and suddenly everyone was the enemy. I realized the thing I relied on for safety actually caused harm, as I no longer needed it. My rage was a weapon built for darker times and through prayer, shadow work, and extensive therapy, I had emerged into the marvelous light of recovery.

And there was my sister standing at the hem of my life, still raging...still bitter...still accusing. Even my old friend avoidance was losing its ability to spare me of my sister's wrath.

Something had to end this lifelong feud.

And then Tommy died.

I'll never forget that day. It was an ordinary day when I drove to the hospice center. The sun was out, and pops of red and yellow flowers danced in a slight breeze.

Tommy had been dealing with a long illness that reduced her body to skin and bones. My plan was to try one more time to convince her she was mistaken about me.

I remember asking to see my sister and being told to follow an attendant down the hall. My thoughts raced in a thousand different directions as I struggled to remember why I came at all. When the door opened, there she was. Dressed in blue, eyes closed, and hands gently clasped together. I reached for one of them, thinking Tommy would open her eyes and pull away like she always did.

The attendant put a hand on my shoulder. "She died this morning not long after breakfast. You are the only visitor she's had in the last few weeks. I'm sure she would have appreciated your company."

I waited for the woman to leave. That my sister died alone raked at a raw place in me. Putting all our differences aside, no one deserved to die alone, not even her.

"I didn't expect this to be the way I would see you again."

Standing in the room alone with her. All the feelings of being this woman's punching bag of a younger sister came barreling to the front of my mind. I thought I would find a satisfaction or guilty pleasure in her illness or death, but a swell of compassion muted any lingering bitterness and resentment. She was at peace, and I felt cheated.

It is my one regret. My sister took her last breath without knowing how much I loved her despite everything that we went through. There would be no deathbed declarations of love, apologies, or overtures of forgiveness. It was just over. The chance to mend fences and that elusive bridge where we stood on opposite ends for a lifetime faded away. Standing in the room with her, the two things I planned to do took on more meaning. Finally, I could let go of her and the painful memories. She'd never hear my ultimate words of forgiveness or goodbye, and I had to be okay with that.

With years of counseling and my ever-growing faith in God, I was.

THE MOMENT I CHOSE ME BY
KAREN STAMPLEY

The Foundation – My Origin Story

I was shaken to my core as I lay in my waterbed one day. Still groggy, my head was pounding, but my heart ached even more. I was dazed, unsure of what was happening to me. As I reached to rub the throbbing pain on the side of my head, a warm liquid drenched my hand. I figured my waterbed must have sprung a leak, but when I tried to roll over from my back onto my side to get up and investigate, pain shot through me so severely that I felt paralyzed. I panicked, as I lay in fear, frozen in place, my eyes darted from side to side.

In a surge of dread, I froze, heart racing, breath shallow, as one haunting thought gripped my mind: What's happening to me? I realized that what covered my hand was not water but my own blood, gushing from a wound in my right temple. I couldn't scream, even as I watched my husband and two young sons arrive home and walk to my bedside. They peered down at me and freaked out when they saw the blood. My husband shouted out in shock, "Oh nooooo! She's dead, with a gunshot wound to her head..."

Our hearts bear the stories of our lives, etched with the marks of our origins, molded by our experiences, scarred by pain, and, if we choose, ultimately rebuilt with truth and faith.

I discovered that the path to becoming a true survivor of life's abuse is marked by five key stages. The first four stages are: Built, Bent, Bruised, and Broken. They often stem from our upbringing, experiences, and the silent wounds we carry.

They can be likened to the four chambers of the heart. We can't always control these four stages, but the final stage, Breakthrough, is a decision, a choice. It is the decision to seek truth, to humble ourselves, to pray, and to intentionally renew our minds. Without this choice, the accumulated damage may lead to a heart overwhelmed by unresolved pain, eventually resulting in spiritual and emotional heart failure.

Each stage tells a part of the story—every wound leaves its mark, and every mark carries a revelation.

My journey was a journey not just of survival, but of uncovering the truth hidden beneath the pain and rising above it.

Just like a physical heart can develop blockages, hardened arteries restricting the flow of life-sustaining blood—our Spiritual Heart, the Survivor's Heart, can become clogged with emotional and spiritual obstructions. Fear, rejection, trauma, and self-deception act as plaque slowly cutting off the ability to give and receive love, to operate in faith, to move freely in purpose. Just as untreated heart disease can lead to heart failure, an untreated, unhealed heart leads to spiritual and emotional collapse.

This is where my transformation truly begins, not in the place of healing, but in the breaking - the place of realization. The realization that the foundation of my heart, though built with purpose, was also gripped with fear and its many characteristics. That my beliefs about myself, my worth, and my purpose were shaped long before I had a say. Before I could ever break through, I had to first understand and penetrate the walls of the fortress that had been built around me.

This is the story of a heart that endured more than it ever

should have. Yet it is not the story of failure or defeat—my story is still unfolding, and the best chapters have yet to be lived.

STAGE 1: BUILT – Pre-Disposition
Framed by Purpose – Formed by Fear

We are infused with genetic traits through the genes we get from our parents. Our family influences everything from physical characteristics to predispositions to certain conditions or structural defects. It is within this stage that the essence of our being is established, setting the stage for how we perceive and respond to the world around us.

As we journey through my story, you'll see how each phase plays a part in shaping my mindset and actions while fracturing my heart along the way—and how I eventually learned to break free from the destructive cycle.

Looking back, I can see that even as a child, I was naturally imaginative, inventive, and full of hope. I saw the world through eyes wide with wonder—optimistic, compassionate, and excited about all that life could be. I was a creative, out-of-the-box thinker who believed in possibilities.

Growing up in a home filled with unwavering tenderness and presence, yet silently ruled by fear, slowly reshaped how I saw the world—from behind the invisible bars of my captivity. My parents, loving and supportive as they were, operated from a place of caution rooted in their own insecurities, and fears which mirrors inadequacies.

Their perspective was shaped by a glass-half-empty outlook—always expecting the worst and bracing for disappointment. There's no blame; they gave me the best of what they knew. Unknowingly, their fear-tinted lens became the lens that shaped my perspective, too. Over time, my heart slowly shifted from fear-less to guarded, from wide open to cautiously hopeful. It learned to dream with limits, to love with a filter, and to shrink itself just enough to feel safe. My heart was positioned not in freedom, but in enduring—still longing, still beating, but no longer fully believing.

Heart Check: My heart was full of hope and optimism; unaware it was already surrounded in quiet captivity. I sensed I was meant for something greater - for myself as well as others - long before I knew that being different would cost me acceptance.

Stage 2: BENT – Childhood
Where Hope Started to Hinge

The way we're raised - shaped by upbringing, family dynamics, and generational beliefs -quietly molds us over time, leaving lasting imprints on the heart. In this phase, the weight of reality begins to twist our inner world, pulling us further from the fullness of who we're meant to be.

As the only girl and youngest of three brothers, I felt like a misplaced puzzle piece—different, misunderstood, and subtly rejected. I watched from the windows or doors as the other kids played joyfully outdoors. Loneliness settled in early, unnoticed and unnamed, and I had no words or tools to fight it.

It certainly didn't help that I looked nothing like my peers - but more like our teachers. I was wrapped in a woman's body before I was ready. I felt like a misfit—too tall, too developed, feet too big— long before I knew what to do with it or age—appropriate styles and sizes were available. Every glance, every comment echoed one message: I didn't fit in.

And sadly, I never even considered that maybe I wasn't supposed to.

To make matters worse, in response to my parents' overprotective choices, people around me began to form inaccurate and unfair perceptions of who they thought I was. The collateral damage was painful—I was misunderstood, and that misunderstanding often led to rejection.

I wasn't allowed to visit neighbors or play at my friends' homes — occasionally, only they could come to mine. That imbalance sparked resentment from some parents, which filtered down to their children. My friends began to echo what they heard at home: "Who does she think she is?" or "Her family thinks they're too good for us—let her stay over there by herself."

It wasn't me, guys. I wanted to belong too. My parents weren't snobs—they were kind and generous neighbors—but fear and limitation shaped their parenting, and I ended up carrying the weight of their caution.

Once again, I suffered in silence, feeling rejected and insignificant.

So, I built a secret fantasy world around my pain, shaped by childhood vows, unspoken longing, and the deep desire to feel valued. Drawn to those who mirrored my ache, I gave more than I was called to—hoping their healing might somehow mend me too.

When that didn't work, I created my own survival plan—one I desperately wanted God to co-sign.

At the time, I didn't understand the difference—or the necessity—of having a personal relationship with Him. I had grown up in church, so I figured I knew enough to assume I was in good spiritual standing. I believed in God, so I thought that meant we were good.

I had heard about Him through my parents' faith, but I didn't truly know Him for myself. Still, I knew His approval mattered. In my childlike reasoning, if I could just get His stamp on my plan, it would be fool-proof—guaranteed success, no heartbreak, no rejection.

So off I go—I imagined the perfect sister to fill the void: a friend, a cheerleader, a safe place. Beneath the fantasy, a veiled sadness was already taking root. I was building my life around what I wished existed—while slowly drifting from what I truly needed to heal.

Heart Check: My heart was hungry for sincere, mutual love—

but instead of speaking that need, for fear of rejection and judgment, I buried it. I abandoned myself in favor of being agreeable and fed on fantasy to survive the ache. The sadness…...

Stage 3: BRUISED – High School
Trapped in a Prison

Trapped in a prison whose walls were first erected by my parents' fear, inadequacies, and overprotective love—I didn't yet recognize the invisible walls that bound me. Their good intentions left a lasting wound, shaping how I saw myself: uncertain, not enough. Over time, those walls were unknowingly fortified by my own growing fears and inner inadequacies. I clung to my own ideas as if they were keys, but they soon became beautifully crafted chains—tightening around the authentic parts of me that were slowly deteriorating.

The accumulated pain and rejection that scar our hearts is where we start recycling our pain—like drinking poison to soothe the wound! Every hurt, every loss, and every instance of rejection begins to form patterns that we believe define us.

Elementary school years had ended. High school arrived like the next act in a long, unfolding drama. Surely this would be where the story changed!

Though somewhat frightened, I looked forward to this new adventure—I was enrolled in an exclusive all-girl high school. I walked into this new chapter expecting to find the sisterhood I had so desperately imagined.

An all-girls school that promised a sanctuary of friendship and belonging—a chance to reimagine the sisterhood I longed for in a target-rich environment where everyone truly understood me. I was ready for a new chapter and determined to take control of my narrative. I quietly longed to be embraced, to be drawn in—not just be present, but truly included and accepted.

I met good friends but still no sisters. My quest continues—I've still yet to find the *Gayle to my Oprah!*

In the corridors of high school, I found that even here, I was still measured by the same old standards. I discovered that while I had good friends, the deep, soul-nourishing connection I had longed for remained elusive. My heart, still tender from childhood, ached for what felt like the missing piece. I was consumed with crafting the perfect plan, never pausing to uncover the truth of who I truly was. My identity remained buried beneath the fantasy I believed would make me whole.

Heart Check (Sister-search High School): The collateral damage to my heart was that I nixed out any possibility of budding lifelong friendships because they didn't line up with my sister saga. "I couldn't see then...I was so attached to the fantasy, I missed the reality growing right in front of me!" God was answering my prayer in "seed form," with those who tried to befriend me in natural, organic ways—versus my "need form," where she would appear magically, fulfilling the perfect sister role I had scripted (no period of growth needed here)!

Transformation Without Truth

Desperate to fill the void yet again, I turned to what "I" thought was a solution—a radical transformation of my outer self. Running out of tricks and time seeming to escape me, my senior year became the stage for Operation External Upgrade.

I believed that if I could just look the part, everything else would fall into place—love, acceptance, worthiness. I thought appearing whole would make me feel whole. I chased external fixes, hoping they'd heal internal wounds, never realizing that true fulfillment wouldn't come from fitting in—but from being aware and rooted in who I was created to be. In trying to become what others would embrace, I became an imposter to my own identity.

I started a healthy weight loss and exercise journey. I worked out with a fierce determination, shed the weight, and reinvented my style. Others started noticing my amazing transformation, but I still didn't see myself...

I knew the scale showed a large reduction, but I still viewed myself through the lens of imperfection and un-fulfillment.

Each time I altered myself to be accepted, I drifted further from the truth of who I was. Beneath the polished image, my heart remained bruised wounded by repeated silence, unmet needs, and misplaced efforts to feel whole. I thought striving for perfection would earn me love and worth, but all it did was deepen the ache and the sadness.

As time went on and I began shopping for my new body, I was stunned—who knew that figure had been hidden underneath? For a moment, it felt like the narrative was shifting. I was seen. Admired. And I thought, "How ya like me now?!"

But the confidence was short-lived. The same inner wounds still sobbed beneath the surface. No matter how much I changed on the outside, the ache inside remained untouched rooted in patterns that a mirror could never fix.

Heart Check (High School): Perfectionism denies progress, and in chasing an ideal, I slowly disconnected from the very process that could have led me to healing—revelation and understanding that I was created on purpose with a purpose!

Fantasy or Fate?

Just two days before graduation, someone new entered my life —kind and intriguing, and full of the qualities I thought I needed. He seemed like the answer to everything I'd been missing. I called him my prince—a welcomed distraction from the ache of the sisterhood that never manifested.

Although I didn't have a real relationship with God yet, I still wanted His approval—on my terms. I felt that Him co-signing my plan would ensure success. I was chasing happiness by any means necessary, convinced that adding someone else to my life would finally bring healing and wholeness to my broken heart. I didn't realize yet that what I wanted wasn't what I truly needed. The deeper truth had not yet found me—and I was unknowingly running in the opposite direction.

Carefully, I built a fortress around him—around the hope that this was finally it. I wrapped our connection in promises and dreams, convinced I was stepping into one of the childhood fantasies I'd held onto for years.

Beyond the longing for a sister, I had always imagined a life of impact, success, and eventually marrying a godly man to build a beautiful family. I believed that if I could just secure this fairytale ending, my broken heart would finally be whole.

What I didn't realize yet was that no dream—no matter how picture-perfect—could heal the parts of me I hadn't yet dared to confront and surrender.

The wedding was beautiful......

But beautiful doesn't mean whole!!!!

Heart Check: Fairy tales are not true. No one was ever coming to rescue me.

Stage 4 – BROKEN – Wife

Hiding in Wife-dumb – (*is a play on the word "wisdom"— describing the silent, gradual loss of self that can happen when a woman pours everything into the roles of wife and mother while unintentionally abandoning her own voice, dreams, and identity. It's not about dishonoring marriage, but about exposing how fear and over-functioning can lead us to hide behind titles instead of standing fully in purpose.*)

Time flew by after the wedding. I began to sense that even this carefully scripted romance was laced with contradictions that I couldn't ignore. I was still searching for validation in everyone else while neglecting the one person I needed most—me.

Fear allowed me to hide in plain sight—trading the dreams and aspirations of a young woman for those of a loving wife and soon-to-be mother.

Don't misunderstand me—this was absolutely one of my most heartfelt desires. I just didn't intend to lose *"me"* in the process.

I was smart—creative, resourceful, and capable. I completed most of the training programs I pursued: beauty school, real estate, transportation service, even a travel business. Despite all that I had gained, I still felt stuck—unable to fully activate my new skills or reach the level of success I desired. The limiting beliefs in my heart were louder than my qualifications. I began to feel like a failure—not because I lacked ability, but because I lacked belief in myself.

Fear convinced me I could only be great with someone beside me—someone to guide me, hype me up, and pull me forward when I felt stuck. My husband, though solid in many ways, couldn't fill that role. I was searching for someone to speak to the doubt within me, to spark what I couldn't yet find in myself.

I had big dreams but kept shrinking them to fit my fear. I placed the weight of my fulfillment on others, expecting them to carry what only God could fill. Though I had wisdom, creativity, and drive, I lacked the courage to lead. So, I stepped aside—again—waiting to be pushed into a purpose I was too afraid to claim.

Fear of failure muted the boldness in me. I looked for affirmation when I needed revelation. And beneath it all, a heaviness stirred—sadness giving way to a slow, settling despair.

Heart Check: I kept placing my dreams in someone else's hands—quietly stepping back from my own voice, my own power, and my own purpose, until I could barely hear myself at all.

BROKEN – Motherhood
Poured Out but Running on Empty

The state of being so overwhelmed by unresolved pain that we end up sabotaging our own lives. This is the turning point—a moment of crisis where the façade finally cracks, revealing the true enemy that has been operating in the shadows.

Six months after the wedding, we excitedly rushed into parenthood—another part of my fantasy story: being a mother—creating someone I could pour all my love into—my baby—and expecting love and joy in return down the line.

When I became a mother, I assumed I would be guaranteed reciprocal love, and an unbreakable bond from infancy well into their adulthood.

These were assignments that I unknowingly gave to my unborn babies—to fill a void in the hopes of guaranteeing the joy of love and acceptance. I thought this would alleviate the childhood pain I hadn't dealt with.

This is the fatal flaw that parents tend to have when we try to give our children what we needed as a child. This robs us of truly learning and meeting the specific needs of our children as individuals.

This plan would ensure that they would never feel my pain. They would be fulfilled! We would be fulfilled!

I was ecstatic when I found out we were expecting our first child. My pregnancy was normal nausea early on, cravings in full swing. We welcomed our first baby, then three more, and my heart was full in many ways. With a husband and four vibrant children, life was busy—and busy became the perfect cover for my hidden pain.

Or so I thought.

Just two weeks before my first child was born, I lost my maternal grandfather—the one I shared a deep, unspoken bond with. His death cracked open the vault of grief I had spent years trying to keep sealed. That long-buried ache didn't whisper—it roared. And with it came an unwelcomed visitor: depression. Bold and uninvited, crashing in like a storm I never saw coming. And I had no umbrella.

I didn't know then what was happening. I had no language for it, no space to process it. So, I carried it—in silence—wearing the weight of depression like an invisible cloak, heavy but hidden. *And the beat goes on…*

Though we had a beautiful family, both my husband and I felt something was missing—a void neither of us could explain. When he began attending his former church, I stayed home more often than not—calling us CME Christians: people who only attended church on Christmas, Mother's Day, and Easter.

I hoped that by his spiritual pursuit, I might somehow feel fulfilled while discarding this heavy weight too. Still, I remained empty. He found some comfort in the attempt. I only found more desolation.

Even after accepting the invitation to his mother's new church, the void persisted. Church felt good on the surface, but it never reached what was broken deep within. Up to that point, nothing—and no-one—had filled the deep abyss in my heart.

Could it be that I was searching for love and acceptance in all the wrong places? In the process, I had lost myself—completely disconnected from God and from myself.

Though I didn't yet know Him intimately, a growing longing for God had begun pulling at me. Something within was awakening—calling me to something greater.

According to the vision I had, my fairytale marriage wasn't fairy-tailing anymore. My husband was stretched thin, my children too young to give back what I'd poured in, and now the heaviness I'd hidden for so long was weighing me down. I had no idea what I was dealing with nor anyone to share with—I just knew I was scared, alone, and exhausted.

Some days, I tried to sleep the ache away...

Then suddenly, *I was shaken to my very core, as I lay in my waterbed. Groggy, panicked, and frozen in fear, I couldn't scream. Astonished, I watched as my husband and two young sons walked through the door and approached my bedside. They peered down at me and freaked out when they saw the blood. My husband shouted out in shock: "Oh nooooo! She's dead with a gunshot wound in her head!"*

That image jolted me straight up—now fully awake. This

dream seemed so real to me in every way. My head fell into my hands, and I began weeping, pleading with God to help me.

What was wrong with me? Why did this vision of suicide appear to me? I'd been struggling intermittently for years with bouts of deep sadness, but at the time I didn't understand the connection to this new escalation.

I just knew after that disturbing daydream that I needed to seek help. Somehow, I knew that this fight was going to be different—very different. It would be the biggest fight of my life, but it would not be a physical one. It would be spiritual. And it would be won or lost *first* in my mind.

This was the moment my soul began to stir—the quiet beginning of my true search for significance. Not in people or performance, but in something deeper… something eternal.

Heart Check: My trauma wasn't my fault, but healing had become my responsibility—not just for me, but for my legacy. I could no longer hide behind distractions. It was time to confront what was breaking me.

STAGE 5 – BREAKTHROUGH
"Buried, But Still Breathing"
BREAKTHROUGH

Breakthrough isn't a moment of rescue—it's a decision to rise. Not just to heal, but to stop shrinking and start showing up. While earlier stages happened to me. THIS one required something from me: action, honesty, and surrender.

Years of people-pleasing and performance—rooted in fear and shaped by an overprotective upbringing—taught me how to exist without fully living. I silenced my voice to be accepted, abandoned my dreams to keep peace, and measured my worth by how well I played the role others needed.

My heart didn't just ache—it slowly disappeared beneath the weight of trying to be enough.

Then came the dream.

I saw myself having taken my own life—a terrifying vision that exposed the toll of unaddressed pain and a lifetime of self-neglect. That moment shook me awake. It wasn't just a nightmare—it was a holy interruption. A divine invitation to do something different.

I realized I was carrying a God-sized ache and placing it in human hands. I was searching for healing in people, applause, and plans I had built out of fear. None of it worked. What I truly needed could only be found in the One who created me.

So, I took the first step.

I began seeking God—not for approval, but for relationship. I started confronting the crippling vows I had made with fear and false identity. And I began discovering and honoring the parts of me I had long ignored.

Self-abandonment had robbed me for decades—through silence, through pretending, through dismissing my own needs as too much. It was birthed from the foundation of my heart, shaped by fear and misperception, and persisted throughout my life.

I had lost sight of myself completely—until I chose to break-through. When I turned back to my Source, He pointed me within. It was only then that my heart began to heal and become whole. In Him, I found not just healing, but myself—and my purpose.

My healing began with small acts of return: praying with honesty, setting boundaries, pursuing joy without guilt, letting God redefine me. It wasn't easy. Healing rarely is. But it's necessary. And I was finally ready!

Awakened into Divine Assignment

As I leaned into my healing, God woke me in the early hours with what I now know was a Divine Liberation Action Plan. He led me to write an exposé—an unmasking of hidden lies and deeply rooted beliefs that had quietly governed my life.

This revelation became the foundation for what He named The Five Steps of Faith. Each step aligned with His Word and became a weapon of truth, empowering me to identify, challenge, and uproot the limiting beliefs that had distorted my identity and sabotaged my purpose. In their place, I began planting truth—His truth.

Through this process, I realized that true healing and transformation couldn't happen without intimacy with God. The Five Steps of Faith revealed the vital importance of knowing Him personally—of building unshakable trust and deep-rooted faith in Him alone.

Transformation came as I renewed my mind. These five steps weren't just principles—they were the path to healing and wholeness. Walking them out in obedience brought freedom to my soul, clarity to my calling, power to my purpose.

It brought restoration to my identity!

Now, I know why I survived.

I have been assigned to help others walk into their healing. This is no longer just my story—it's my mission. My purpose.

The Five Steps of Faith is now a book designed to guide others toward healing and wholeness in transforming their mind and heart!

This was His divine plan for me all along.

Wholeness didn't come all at once. It came with each small, defiant decision—to stop waiting and start walking. To stop performing for approval and start becoming who I was always meant to be.

I wasn't rescuing myself. I was finally surrendering and partnering with the One who could.

The Five Steps of Faith became my blueprint for healing. This God-given methodology didn't just help me renew my mind; it exposed the hidden grip of self-abandonment that had ruled my life for far too long.

I had spent years showing up for others while silently erasing myself- shrinking, deferring, silencing my voice, my dreams, and my needs. But step by step, God taught me how to stand in truth, how to value the woman He created, and how to stop leaving myself behind.

Now, I live with a Survivor's Heart. Not because I avoided pain, but because I stopped letting it define and control me.

I am no longer the girl who disappeared.

I am the woman who came back for her.

I. Chose. Me.

I am a champion.

Rebuilding. Restoring. Becoming. Thriving.

Heart Check: This time, I didn't wait for someone else to choose me, I chose myself. I faced the fear, confronted the lies, and reached for God with everything I had left.

My healing didn't begin with a miracle; it began with a decision. A decision to no longer abandon the woman I was called to be!

And that choice *changed everything*!

SURVIVING ME: A HARD LOOK IN THE MIRROR BY LA AMMITAI

even, eight, nine... that is the day my second child was born. Initially, the numbers of his date of birth didn't mean much to me. I was just excited that my baby boy was finally here. But never would have fathomed what was to come five months later.

Earth-shattering screams, belting cries, and blaring sirens penetrated my ears on the morning of December 26. I opened my eyes and rose to my feet from bed. There my mother was, holding him out to me screaming, "help him!"

I quickly swooped him in the cuffs of my biceps and curled him tightly against my chest. Without regard to the beating my knees would take, I plunged to the floor and laid his cold, stiff body on my rigid bedroom floor. The only padding that rested between him and the concrete was a wafer-thin sheet of carpet. I leaned over him, my lips pressing against his—praying that my breaths became his.

The thumping footsteps of my fiancé pacing back and forth gave me a rhythm to follow as I continued CPR. It helped to drown out the flood of uncontrollable emotional screams whaling from my mother's lips. The sirens in the distance temporarily restored my faith. Help was on the way. But the louder the sirens became, the longer it seemed for help to arrive. "What the hell is taking so long. Where are they?"

One-two-three-four-five-six-seven-eight-nine—exhale, exhale. Repeat. I refused to stop resuscitation until paramedics arrived. His erratic movements suggested he was coming back, but it was just my breath leaving his body. Still, I kept going.

The frantic pounding down the stairwell leading to my bedroom gave me just a little more hope. The paramedics had arrived. EMT's swarmed in pulling me off him and swiftly taking him away.

I remember walking past an officer on the stairwell to hear him utter, "How could she...?" The rage that shot through my body upon hearing those condemning words come out of his mouth was something like I had never felt before.

How could he blame me? Why was this my fault? But I had no time to wallow in that status as the paramedics were loading my son into the ambulance. I had no time for callous questions or statements. My only concern was getting to the hospital with him and praying and hoping that the nurses and doctors could save his life.

He earned his wings later that morning. I was devastated, crumbled, confused, frustrated... You know, half of the time I didn't even know how to feel. It all seemed too surreal. A parent's worst nightmare is outliving their child. That became a heart-wrenching reality. How could this happen to me? Why did this happen to me?

The word of what happened to Kylon spread quickly throughout my family and friends. They drove in from all over to show their love and support. My heart was hurting and my mind was spacey. I barely remember much from that day proceeding the doctor calling out his time death. I couldn't figure out whether I was coming or going, let alone experience anything in the present moment. They say the present is a gift. It was more like a curse and nightmare for me.

The most heart wrenching call I had to make was to his father. I could barely make out the words as I stuttered and cried through telling him what happened. Before I could tell him the entire story, he was off the phone racing through the streets of Decatur with God knows what thoughts running through his mind. I prayed for his sanity and safe arrival. "Peace be still! God, we need you right now! Lord, I pray for his mind and his heart. I'm so sorry. Help us, Father. God, I pray for the safety of those who cross his path on the way here. Oh, keep us, Lord. Peace be still. Peace be still. Peace be still."

When he arrived at the hospital, his face was flush with anger, sadness, and confusion. He was crushed. Eyes of rage pierced through my fiancé's entire being. "I'm going to kill him! I know this is all his fault! What is he even doing here?" The heavy police presence was the only thing that kept this from becoming a war zone with multiple casualties.

The reflections of our love triangle weighed heavily on me in that very moment. The guilt and shame crept in like a category-3 hurricane. It engulfed me. The *what if's* and *if I would have just* flooded my convictions. I cried every tear I had in me, then shock took over. I became zombie-like in nature as I began to internally deteriorate.

Where it All Started:

"Hey sis. Where you at?" My nosey little sister was always in my business.

"I'm just out taking a drive. What's up?"

"Come home quick. I've got some friends over and my guy has a buddy that wants to meet you."

My sister is six years younger than me, so the thought of any of her friends taking a romantic liking to me kind of made my skin crawl. "Girl, I'm grown as hell. I'm not coming home to kick it with some young dude.

"He's not young. He's around your age. He gave my friends a ride and I told him about you. He's fine as hell. Just come on before he leaves."

I arrived home to find out that my sister wasn't lying. He was, indeed, fine as hell. A tall, thin-framed, light-skinned man, with a long bushy mane pulled back in a ponytail stood before me in my living room. It was the rough-around-the-edges look that sealed the deal for me. I was a sucker for a sexy hood gentleman.

"I don't know where you've been all my life, but I'll be sure as hell to keep you if

you let me have you." The top row of teeth met his bottom lip as his hazel eyes pierced into the depths of my soul. I was hooked before I even knew much of anything about him. Lust snuck its way in and took the wheel of destiny.

In the streets, he was known as Fang. He worked at a fast-food restaurant and didn't have a driver's license. That should have been my first red flag. Yet, I had seen so much more potential in him. I don't know what it is with some of us women who think we can just change a man into what we desire him to be. Yeah, I was one of those.

A fast-food gig wasn't going to cut it. I'm a small-town girl with big dreams, and I need my man's pockets to be deep to fulfill my life desires. So, I created a resume for him, freshened up his appearance a bit, and tickled his intellect... along with a few other things. He soon landed a second job making three times as much on the other job.

Fang quickly recognized my fire, that's for sure. I had a vision for the life I desired, and I knew just how to get there. I had that man wrapped around my finger. He was alll about me, worshipping the ground I walked on. Things were working out just as I planned and nobody could tell me a damn thing.

Suddenly, it all came tumbling down. The too-good-to-be-true syndrome kicked in amidst our first big argument. I was triggered. The memories of my ex-husband began to haunt me. The abuse, the lies, the betrayal...they had a strong hold on me. It had me feeling like my head was in the clouds with this man and at any moment my heart would plummet to the ground, the hardest fall and break imaginable. Maybe I over-reacted...but I sure as hell didn't wait around to find out. I ended it just as quick as we started it.

Three weeks later, I met MJ. He was the wingman between my best friend and her guy at the time. Since Fang and I were no longer a thing, I didn't mind hanging out with him on a double-date. I was honest and upfront with him about my past relationships and disclosed to him that I had no desire to start another. We agreed that a no-strings-attached ordeal would fit the bill. Another three weeks later, two blue lines appeared on a pregnancy test.

It only seemed logical to redact the no-strings-attached arrangement and attempt to make the family thing work with MJ. He was very clear that he didn't want just another baby-mama—seven children and five mothers were enough. Unfortunately, things took a turn for the worse for him financially and he struggled to get a grip on life. I tried to offer him comfort and counsel, but he just couldn't pull it together. There was no way I was going to allow a man to lead me into destruction with him. I could do bad all by myself with the one autistic child I had already and the unexpected one that was growing daily in my womb.

The chaotic fling between MJ and I lead me right back into the arms of the man I ran away from ... Fang. And like a knight in shining armor, he came to swoon me back into his graces. I can't lie, the opportunity to roll the dice again had me daydreaming about what finally could be. However, I wasn't sure how well he would receive the fact that I was with child.

Learning about my pregnancy definitively took him by surprise. He even questioned if I was sure that it wasn't his. With respect to the conception timeline, we had only been split for three weeks. That was enough to create an inkling of doubt in paternity.

Regardless on the circumstance, he was there for me, waiting on me hand and foot, just as he was before. He assured me that no matter the outcome of paternity, he was right where he wanted to be. He was committed to loving me and raising a family with me and my soon to be two children.

I fell in love with the idea of a complete family. I already had one failed marriage; I didn't want another broken home. Conversations of marriage (again) and more children had me praying that he was my child's father.

On July 8, 2009, 5 pounds and 14 oz of love erupted from my womb. Weeks after giving birth I ordered a DIY paternity kit. With one swab of my Fang's cheek and another swab from Kylon's, the samples were mailed off to the lab.

Two weeks later, I received an email from the DNA diagnostic company. The thought of opening it had my body perspiring and filled with anxiety. I closed my eyes and took a deep breath.

Click. I opened the email. My eyes buck-wide, scanning the letter frantically in search of the answer I was hoping for. Instead, disappointment greeted me. 99.9% NOT the father.

I can't say that I was shocked. Deep down I knew that Fang wasn't the father, but I was hopeful. I had just gotten wrapped up in the idea of getting back with him, the child being his, getting married, and living happily ever after.

No matter the outcome, I'm where I want to be. Fang's declaration of love and devotion rang in my head. I still couldn't chance it, however. I convinced him, which didn't take much, that he was Kylon's father. We got engaged and I got my *happily ever after ...* so I thought.

In October 2009, we got into a huge argument. We had been experiencing some very difficult times. And when things got heated between us, it got very ugly. That man's tongue was a sharp blade that pierced my heart. When it came to the tit-for-tat, I wasn't short-stopping either. I struck back with one of the lowest blows a man can take.

"If you want out, you can leave. Kylon is not yours anyways."

The room became so silent you could only hear the fan spinning in the near distance. He picked up his coat and walked out of the door. I assumed he was going to blow off some steam and would be right back. At first, hours went by. Then, days.

Fang finally called about a week later. We had a serious heart-to-heart. I felt so terrible. I hurt him, again. We agreed it would be best to inform MJ and do the paternity testing the right way this time, through the courts. This way, there would be no possible tampering of evidence.

MJ was excited to hear the possibility of him being Kylon's father was still on the table. He even tried using it to leverage any chance of us getting back together. That wasn't happening.

In November 2009, the results were in. MJ was 99.9% THE FATHER.

One month later, Kylon passed.

Kylon was laid to rest on the blistering cold and snowy day of December 29th. As we remembered him in a beautiful church service, nothing short of unconditional love filled my heart. As much as I wanted to sob and mope, my spirit wouldn't let me. Instead, I danced, shouted, and twirled with my hands raised to God giving thanks for his short-lived existence as the praise team sang his home-going song.

The final stop... Greenwood Cemetery. I chose Greenwood over the other local resting places because Kylon's last name was Greenwood (no coalition or relation to the cemetery). It just seemed fitting.

As he was lowered into his resting place six feet under the cold and wet ground, I exhaled. Little did I know, the nightmare had only just begun. This was only the first time that I would bury him.

THE CEMETERY SCANDAL

Some time passed and summer rolled around quickly. Reality was finally starting to set in. It was time to put the finishing touches on Kylon's burial plot. Due to the harsh winter weather and unsettled ground just months before, the cemetery officials advised I wait until spring or summer to purchase a headstone. That time had come.

On June 7, 2010, I visited Decatur Monument Works. A pale woman with bone straight, sandy brown hair greeted me. "Hi, how can I help you?", she asked.

I swallowed before responding, "I'm here to purchase a headstone for my child's gravesite", I said in shaky voice.

She immediately offered her condolences and followed up with a series of questions. I had no idea there were so many decisions to make.

I learned that the cemetery he was buried in has sections that only allow for certain grave markers. Apparently, I was ill-prepared. I didn't bring any paperwork with me to the monument shop to verify his exact location at Greenwood cemetery. However, she assured me that all was well.

"That's ok, the resolution is just a phone call away. I will call Greenwood to verify." She asked for Kylon's full name, date of birth, and date of death.

Seven, eight, nine. (07/08/09)

She made the call to Greenwood Cemetery. I waited patiently in the chair across from her desk. Listening in to her conversation with the cemetery manager, I was anxiously hoping that I would be allowed to mark his plot with a huge upright teddy bear stone. I really liked that one for him.

Just when I thought her face couldn't get any paler, it did. She slowly places the phone on hold. Silence rang across the room for about sixty seconds—but it felt more like sixty minutes.

With a flushed and flustered look on her face she stumbled across her words, "They want me to ask you...they want me to ask you, are you sure this is where you buried your son because they don't have any records of him?"

The horror film I had been starring in became a sequel.

Rightfully so, for a split moment, I lost my mind. The earth-shattering screams and belting cries from the morning of December 26th rang in my head all over again as I mimicked them in real time.

I bolted out the door and ran to my car. Driving away frantically at high speeds, I raced to my mother's house. In moments where I don't know what to do, she always seemed to have the answers. However, I knew in my heart that this was one she wasn't going to be able to fix. I still needed her love.

I could barely speak while attempting to give her the news. As strong as I had been through this entire experience, the weight became too heavy to bare. My emotions swiftly shifted from anger and rage to sadness and gut-wrenching pain. Life in that moment didn't seem worth living anymore. I was ready to end it all.

My mother convinced me to seek help. She called 911 for a voluntary admission to psych. Once we arrived at the local hospital, St. Mary's, the doctors came in to assess me. They spoke a preliminary plan of treatment that included strong doses of anti-depressants and electroconvulsive (electro-shock/ECT) therapy to alter my brain waves.

I was terrified. What the hell did I just sign up for? I am not crazy! This is not what I want! They can't do this! And to my relief...they couldn't. Unbeknownst to me, I was pregnant. Be-nadryl to help me sleep at night and in-house therapy sessions was all the doctors could prescribe for my treatment plan. Saved by the womb.

Meanwhile, my mother worked very hard behind the scenes to get answers from the cemetery manager, Town Hall, and police detectives. It even went as far as court hearings.

My family came to see me every day to show me love and

support. My mother kept me updated on the information involving the case of my missing/misplaced child.

The audacity of the cemetery to present my family with an excel spreadsheet marked with an *X* in one of the cells to represent where my son was buried was diabolical. On this very same sheet of paper, every other cellblock had the last name of the deceased written plainly and boldly. The disrespect of *X marks the spot* was enough for me to lose my mind twice.

At the court hearing, the judge wasn't convinced either. An order of exhumation was granted. That's when I knew that my time at the hospital had reached an end. There was absolutely no way that I would allow them to proceed in my absence.

Upon meeting with the doctor, I updated him with breaking news of the exhumation date. July 26, 2010. With a sense of urgency, I requested release of custody. I had to be there.

"I have reviewed your file and spoke with your therapist. She says you've been doing great in individual and group therapy. However, while I empathize with your situation, I still don't think you're quite ready to be released," he explained.

I squinted my eyes at him furiously. In my most graceful voice I replied, "Let me explain something to you doc... I'm sad, mad, hurt, deeply in pain, angry, and damn sure outraged. But one thing that I am not, is fucking crazy. Put yourself in my shoes. What if this were your child, your family? How would you react? Are your feelings justified then? So, listen ... we can do this the easy way, or we can do this the hard way. You can sign the papers for my release, and I will go be with my family for my son's exhumation, —or I will tear this motherfucker up and show you real crazy. And there won't be a damn thing you can do about it because I'm pregnant."

I sat back in my chair, arms and legs crossed, awaiting his reply.

"Ok, on one condition. I am requesting that you seek outpatient therapy no later than one week upon release."

I smugly agreed. The secretary drew up the paperwork. We

both signed on the dotted line. I was released from the hospital to be with my family just before the exhumation.

On the morning of July 26, 2010 we gathered at the cemetery in hopes of locating my baby. I stood there just staring at the workers as they dug and dug. I could feel my heart in the pit of my stomach. The NAACP and local news officials surrounded the area.

The moment came; they found a small casket.

I held my hands in prayer as they raised it to ground level. I was in no mental condition to receive more traumatic news. I needed, more than anything, for this to be my baby. A cemetery worker opened the casket. A family friend peered inside. He turned to me and with a gentle head nod and confirmed that my baby boy had been found.

Graceland, another local cemetery contacted me immediately. They gave their condolences and wanted nothing more than to make it right on behalf of the city. They offered a second burial ceremony to include a headstone for Kylon, free of charge. Following the release of two white doves in the sky, he was home in his final resting place.

Seven. Eight. Nine... The digits that signaled both the ultimate heartbreak and my spiritual awakening.

Reflection Connection

When life seemingly hands us lemons, it's not always to make lemonade. At some point, we must take a hard look in the mirror and own our energy. My reflection in the mirror was toxic, deceitful, manipulative, self-serving, and ungodly. Once I was able to see myself, I couldn't unsee it. They say real change happens when you finally get sick of your own shit. And I was beyond sick and tired. I fell to my knees and surrendered to God.

On my journey of self-awareness, self-discovery, and healing God revealed to me my connection reflections. He showed me that every person and thing in my life served a deeper why and purpose ... like my children, for instance. I discovered who I was becoming and how I was designed to serve through my children.

My oldest son, Camerson, who has Autism Spectrum Disorder (ASD), has a fascination with numbers. His connection with numbers is intricate and complex. One day, while leaning back in my recliner and wallowing in the aftermath of two failed divorces, abusive relationships, unemployment, and the loss of a child, my attention was called to the red, blue, and green Lego pattern in the middle of my living room.

Every day, for at least thirty consecutive days, he covered the floor with the same design. When he finished his daily pattern, he placed the numbers 2-3-4-9-4-2 right next to it with refrigerator magnets. Curiosity kicked in and I googled the numerical sequence. I was taken aback.

234942 is a hex color code containing 14% Red, 29% Green, and 26% Blue. A beautiful representation of the Legos I played hopscotch over daily in my living room. The revelation that there might be a more profound reason he placed that specific Lego pattern on my living room floor led to me to research the deeper meanings of numbers. That's when numerology found me. I, in turn, found myself.

I was so accustomed to weaving my reality around other's lives that I didn't recognize who I was at first. My *Numerology Soul Blueprint* reconnected me with my inner child. It revealed my hidden gifts and forgotten passions. I started to fall in love with my most authentic self—a feeling I had never felt before. That's when God called me to devote thirty days to myself with the promise of liberation from the shackles I had bound myself with. I answered the call ... but I charter the territory alone.

February 2020, eleven women joined me on a virtual *ME-journey*. We met on Zoom every day for thirty days. It the most raw and realest experience that I've ever encountered. We laughed together. We cried together. We even belted out screams when needed. It was the safest space without judgement. Our healing process included daily affirmations, music therapy, neuro-linguistic programming (NLP) practices, numerology principles, meditation, and journaling. A true sisterhood was formed. In 2022, the thirty-day *ME-journey* became a #1 bestselling book.

30 Days of Me: A Kickstart to Your Inner Healing Journey has aided many women across the globe on their self-discovery and personal development journey. It's more than just a book, it's a movement—a life-long *Me vs. Me* journey. The main color of the cover was inspired by color-code *234942*, the code that once laid on my living room floor.

As a result of reflections of Kylon, I now live by the *seven (7)*, *eight(8)*, *nine (9)* principle. In numerology, the numerical message decodes as follows:

Seven (7) – Quest for the deeper meanings to life and discover who you are.

Eight (8) – Own your energy and the authority over your innate God-given gifts.

Nine (9) – Surrender to the sacrifice. Every beginning has an ending. What are you willing to let go of?

Take a hard look in the mirror. If you don't like what you see, create a new reflection. Everything you need is already inside you.

OWNING MY POWER: HOW I BROKE FREE FROM OPINIONS AND LABELS BY U.M. HIRAM

*J*n the Beginning

Coo-Coo.
Crazy.
Dingy.
Fool.

A few of the words I heard people, including family members, use to describe my mother. The beautiful, light, brown-skinned woman had a smile as bright as the sparkle of a diamond. Being middle school age at the time, I didn't comprehend how those labels were derogatory and mean. She dealt with bouts of schizophrenia, and it made some folks feel that they could place all kinds of labels on her. This mental illness is something that she battled with for several years.

It was sad that her battle with mental illness overshadowed the good she did and the kindness she showed to many throughout the years. She loved to cook and feed people, especially her desserts. Baking cakes seemed to be one of her favorite things to do—butter pecan, German chocolate, and pound cake with vanilla icing.

Unfortunately, my sister and I had front row seats to her manic episodes - the hallucinations and hospitalizations. Tears streamed as I watched the woman that I loved beyond measure transform into someone scary. Through all of that, she managed to take medications for her illness, saw a psychiatrist regularly, made sure her girls were taken care of, and found more stability when we left New York.

Watching the Big Apple fade in the distance as we crossed the George Washington Bridge and the Hudson River, realization set in that we were heading to the Deep South to stay for good. It had been in the works for a few months due to my mom's challenges with mental illness and doing the best she could to raise her two girls.

My grandmother and a few close relatives felt it best to move us out of the big city and reside in the country, where we would have added support. Honestly, I think they were concerned and didn't want anything to happen to her or us, even though we had family living in New York.

Reflecting on my conversation years ago with my mom, it reminded me of how terrified I was about the change.

"Mommy, do we have to go live in the country with Grandma?"

"Yes, baby," she said. "Everything will be all right."

"But I won't have any friends. All of them will still be in the city."

"You will make new friends, and you have a lot of cousins down south."

"I know, but will they like me?" I asked.

She smiled. "Yes, they will love you just like I do."

No more returning from summer visits to the city I called home for years, traveling on Interstate 95—nothing but dirt roads, fields, farm animals, and all things country living. I enjoyed spending summers in the country, but I always looked forward to returning to New York. Lights, sounds, Chinese food, and my friends, plus all the activities I loved participating in.

Growing up, I had plenty of things that I wanted to do...be an actor, dancer, musician, singer, etc. While attending junior high school in New York, I played several instruments like the clarinet, piano, and steel drums. Additionally, I was able to act in a select few school plays—my most memorable being cast as one of the lead characters in "Purlie."

Nothing was going to change the decision that was made, so I sat back and watched the road. Ten hours, my brain was filled with so many thoughts. I wondered if I'd be able to make new friends in high school and make solid connections with my family that lived in South Carolina. I felt emotional and anxious when we reached the South of the Border, a famous landmark two hours away from where we were heading.

Traveling down the three-mile curvy dirt road affectionately named Crane Pond, to my grandmother's house, I glanced at the private school sitting to the left before we rounded the first curve. Two miles down the road, acres of cotton and corn fields were on the right, where the owner and his family farmed. One of our family's close friends' home was directly across from where they grew snap peas, green beans, and watermelons on the land adjacent to him.

Less than one-half mile up on the right, the yellow house appeared, where we would spend the next few years. It took a little while for me to get used to the difference in sounds and the fact that we were living in the country, surrounded by trees and wide-open spaces. I remembered a brief conversation I had with my grandmother while we were settling in.

"Grandma, are we going to stay with you forever?" I asked with tears in my eyes that I didn't allow to stream down my face, afraid that I would get in trouble for being so emotional.

She looked at me and replied, "Yes, girl, fix your face."

Sniffling, I said. "Yes, ma'am."

She was a caring yet intimidating woman who believed children should only be seen and not heard. Just follow what you were told and don't ask any questions. It's the same formula she used to raise her children, and one that kept me in a timid place for several years. Fearful was one of the labels that I wore for a long time.

BECOMING **Who I Am**

AS SOON AS we learn to talk, people start giving us labels. Some can be deemed as harmless, such as shy, smart, athletic. However, others can be hurtful where words like *troublemaker, too sensitive or not good enough, are used to describe someone. These labels affect how others view us, and, more importantly, how we see ourselves."*

I'd like to take you on a brief journey with some of the labels placed on me growing up. In kindergarten, I was the "quiet kid". I didn't raise my hand, not because I didn't know the answer, but because I was afraid of giving the wrong answer or being embarrassed. As a result of that, my teacher told my mother, *"I lacked confidence"*.

From that moment on, "insecure" became a word used to describe me, even when I was simply thoughtful or observant. I wore that label like an invisible cape, and any label worn too long starts to blend into your identity.

As I matured, more labels materialized. In middle school, I was *awkward* and a *nerd.* In high school, *plain, too skinny,* and *high yellow wannabe*—that is just three of the names I will share because I won't give the other labels any traction or power. No matter how many times I tried to redefine myself, someone was always ready to remind me who I was *supposed* to be, as far as they were concerned.

"So, you think you are cute just because you are light-skinned," one girl said. *"You are not."*

"You look just like your momma, and you will be crazy just like her." That came out of the mouth of a close relative. How hurtful is that?

What I didn't realize then was how much power I had already given away by accepting labels as if they were true. When you are young and impressionable, you often absorb things that are said *to you*—at least I did. At the end of the day, labels were created to reduce the importance of a person and paint a perspective that isn't necessarily correct.

The hardest labels to shake are the ones placed on us when we are young. Childhood impressions can have a lasting effect that stretches into adulthood, causing many of our struggles with self-identity.

Another example was being told I wasn't "leadership material." I was quiet, yes, but that didn't mean I lacked vision or strength. I internalized the label and avoided every opportunity to lead. It wasn't until the military in my early twenties that I didn't have a choice but to be catapulted into that type of role. It created an epiphany for me, realizing I'd been living under other people's assumptions for years.

Shedding these early labels takes intentional effort. It takes unpacking, reflecting, embracing your growth, and considering who those labels came from. It means asking yourself—Is this who I am, or who I was told I am? Also, realizing that those individuals were probably dealing with their own shortcomings, the coping mechanism for them was to project by showing negativity to you.

Unfortunately, the world doesn't stop assigning labels when you grow up. In adulthood, the labeling becomes subtle, but no less damaging. Those labels are often tied to your job title, income bracket, relationship status, race, gender, or how you parent your children. You become:

underachiever

overachiever
too ambitious
single and lonely
too loud
too quiet
too much of something.

Any of that sound familiar?

The workplace can be notorious for labeling. Ever been called *difficult* just for advocating for yourself? Or *too emotional* for expressing your frustration? These are not personality flaws; they are often coded responses to people stepping outside the comfort zones of others.

To reject these adult labels requires boundaries and courage. It means learning the difference between feedback and projection. Not every opinion is the truth. Not every critique is useful. People will try to define you in terms that make sense to them, not necessarily to you, so don't allow any of that to penetrate your spirit.

It helps to have an internal compass: values, vision, and a sense of purpose that are independent of public perception. If you know who you are, you won't need the world to co-sign on anything.

There is tremendous power in rewriting your story. This doesn't mean pretending things didn't happen or ignoring past identities—it means permitting yourself to evolve.

"I, Unique Hiram, do solemnly swear that I will support and defend the Constitution of the United States against all enemies, foreign and domestic; that I will bear true faith and allegiance to the same..." For anyone who has ever spoken these words, like me, it changes your life forever. It became the catalyst to realizing the resiliency, intelligence, and leadership traits that were always within me.

Having the opportunity to grow as a person and being placed in positions to lead as well as mentor others while navigating this stage in my life was refreshing and freeing. It was the difference in recognizing who people thought I was and reclaiming my true identity. Serving 21 years in the United States Navy was a lifesaving, character-building, and amazing experience that I wouldn't alter. Every day wasn't always sunshine and roses, but it allowed me to shed the labels that tried to keep me in bondage.

I would challenge you to ask yourself—what labels have I accepted that no longer fit? Who would I be without them?

You get to decide. Not your elementary teacher. Not your family. Not your ex.

You are not the worst thing someone has ever said about you. You are not confined by the imagination and negativity of others.

One of my favorite scriptures is

> *"I will praise thee; for I am fearfully and wonderfully made: marvellous are thy works; and that my soul knoweth right well."*
> (Psalm 139:14 KJV)

You are allowed to grow out of boxes. You are allowed to surprise people. You are allowed to be both fierce and kind, quiet and powerful, broken and still brilliant.

The labels may keep coming. That's okay. Let them.

Because you are *not* a label. You are a story still unfolding.

SINGLE MOM to Entrepreneur

IN SEPTEMBER 1990, at the age of 20, I became a mom. Let's talk about life-altering and, of course, the labels that followed this chapter in my life. Here are some of the things that were spoken about me:

"She messed up her life and won't amount to anything now"

"She won't be able to take care of her baby", and

"How could she be so stupid?"

Unfortunately, the moment a woman becomes a young, single

mother, the world hands you a host of labels before they ever ask your name.

Irresponsible.

Promiscuous.

Welfare Queen

Uneducated

THESE LABELS ARE CRUEL, narrow-minded, and often far from the truth. But they are handed out as freely as someone's opinion.

My mother used to share this with my sister and I. "Opinions are like a$$holes, everyone has them." At the end of the day, it is a true statement because people feel they are entitled to provide their input about your life, famous, infamous, or not.

I have learned from first-hand experience that for young mothers, the judgment begins even before the baby is born. People whisper behind your back, speak failure over your life, and question your worth. Society paints a picture of the single mother as someone who "did things the wrong way," and this narrative overshadows everything else. You might be resilient, resourceful, loving, and determined to do meaningful things in life, but the truth is, people will often see you through their own misguided assumptions, not the truth of who you are. Don't let that dim your light.

Even though I had already graduated from high school and was taking classes at a community college, my mother was upset when I got pregnant. Her disappointment and the way she displayed it cut me to the core of my being.

"I knew you were a fast-tailed girl," she spoke with venom rolling off her tongue. *"You have messed up your life."*

This moment will forever be etched in my mind because it was contentious and hurtful. I remember feeling like I had huge weights sitting on my shoulders, along with wondering if I could be a good mother to my child. I was young and didn't have a clue about what the future would hold for us.

Labels like "single mom" are often loaded with assumptions. Rarely do people associate those words with leadership, time management, or emotional intelligence. Yet, raising a child alone demands all of those and more. It means making every decision and bearing every burden. But still having to show up, day after day, for someone who depends on you completely. To carry that weight while being underestimated is terrifying and a quiet form of heroism.

Young single mothers face a unique challenge: not only are we raising children, but we are also raising ourselves and growing into adulthood under the microscope of judgment. Every mistake is magnified. Every triumph is dismissed. It's a reality that requires strength, grace, and sacrifice.

Having to decide what would be best for my son and me led to my joining the military. I wanted to provide a life for him that was stable and in a different environment away from South Carolina. As an initial sacrifice, I asked my mother to be his guardian and provided a temporary power of attorney while I went to boot camp in Orlando, Florida, and then on to my first duty station in Norfolk, Virginia.

After securing off-base housing and childcare, I brought him with me permanently. With him being young, it was an interesting transition because he had spent so much time living with my mom. I didn't get to see him take his first steps; that stays etched in my mind. I promised I would not miss any other important milestones if I could help it.

I reflect on the conversation that I had with my mother when it was time to make the transition with him staying with me full-time.

"Nique, are you sure that you will be able to handle having Malc with you?" she asked.

"Yes, ma'am. Everything is set up for him to be in Virginia."

"That is such a long way from here."

Looking at her, it seemed ironic how mad she was when I had gotten pregnant. Now, here she was with the onset of separation anxiety with her grandson. I understood because it was the same way I felt when I had to leave him with her.

"Mom, we are not that far away," I replied. "You can come see us, and we will visit when we can."

"But you don't know those people," she whispered, glancing over at the wooden curio cabinet, then at my son watching television.

"Mommy, it's going to be fine. I promise."

Reaching across the dining room table, I grabbed her hand for reassurance. As if on cue, Malcolm hopped up from the chair and walked over to give her the biggest hug. His little arms gave her the peace that my mere words alone couldn't right then.

If you are a single mother, know that someone's label that they try to place on you does not determine your destiny. Being a single parent is not a limitation; it's a chapter in your journey. It does not mean that life is over. It's one part of your story, not the whole picture.

You are not "less than." You are a woman who chose love and responsibility when others might have walked away. It is not a mistake that you were chosen to take this walk in life.

As I look back over my life and all that I've been able to experience as well as accomplish, it blows my mind. Retiring from the military, having media coverage opportunities in the NASCAR industry, making strides as an HR professional, becoming an entrepreneur, and a bestselling author. Doing all of this as a single mother, debunking those labels that were meant to derail all of these wonderful life experiences.

Yes, there were challenging days, but through it all, I know that I was built for this journey. I would encourage you to realize and embrace this.

One of the scriptures that I hold dear and referred to during those times is

*"I will lift up mine eyes unto the hills, from whence
cometh my help. My help cometh from the Lord,
which made heaven and earth."* (Psalm 121: 1-2 KJV)

Rewriting the narrative of my life and shedding those labels started with me refusing to shrink. Owning my story and sharing it is so empowering. I would encourage you to challenge false assumptions by simply being who you are boldly and unapologetically. Let those around you see what strength looks like, not because you hid your struggle, but because you lived your absolute truth.

Know that you are not just a *"single mom."*

You are a provider. A protector. A nurturer. A dreamer. A builder. A healer. And no matter what the world says, you are worthy of every good thing that comes into your life. You are deserving. Never let someone else's limited vocabulary become the language of your life.

You are more than a label. You are a *masterpiece*!

FROM HEARTACHE TO HEART LED
BY DANIELLE DETIEGE

*M*y grandmother would say, "You better put gravy on my name!" in the same way today we say, "Put some respect on my name."

My journey starts with Mrs. Hazel Burbank, my grandmother. She had the biggest heart of anyone I have ever met. She was the matriarch of our family and most of the families she was connected to. No one ever went unfed in her presence, and it seemed like she adopted every person in need she encountered.

My grandmother held a very special place in my heart because she was not only my grandma, but she also stepped in to raise me when I lost my mother when I was six years old. My mother's final words were for my grandmother to take care of me, and Grandma took the promise she made very seriously. She retired and took on raising me full time.

When I was little, I saw her as this strong stern serious woman, not to be played with. As serious as she was, Grandma was always able to make everything around her better than she found it. As I got older, our relationship transitioned from parent and child to one that was more like a friendship.

I looked forward to our daily conversations, and talking mess about any and everyone. She was so smart, witty, and funny! I have so many memorable moments and quotes living rent free in my head.

One of my favorite exchanges was when she asked, "What channel is it on?" When I told her the The Republican Convention was on PBS, she remarked "That can't be right. Ain't no way they putting Trump on the educational channel!"

That was her. Always leaving you with a full belly and a smile no matter how you came to her. She was a huge piece of my heart! After I had my son, Noah, our relationship shifted once again. Not on my end, I still held her in the same place. But she had demoted me to Noah's transportation to her. I was now the vehicle to get my son to her. I was no longer greeted with "hello" or "how are you?", it was now "where's Noah?"

I gave her grace because she called dibs on him from birth and often reminded me that he was *her* child! Their relationship was beautiful. He never got the stern lady of my childhood. He only got sweetness and compassion. So, of course, only he could finally convince her to go to the doctor after falling several times. The rest of the family pleaded with her to see a doctor but all he had to do was look her in the eyes and ask and she said yes.

None of us expected a doctor's appointment to turn into an immediate admission to the hospital. In a matter of hours, my life was completely shaken up. The woman with the biggest heart I knew, was diagnosed with congestive heart failure. And her doctor believed that she had been walking around with it for over 20 years! My grandmother, who hadn't been to a doctor since she had her last child, was now in the hospital. I immediately began taking shifts alternating nights with my aunt.

I would spend the night, get up at 6:00 a.m. to drive home, take a shower, get my son ready for school, drop him off, and return to the hospital to sit with her during the day until my aunt came. Once we traded places, I would go home to cook dinner and lay in my husband's arms on the sofa until bedtime. Then we would do it all over again the next day switching places again, so someone was always with Grandma.

That was what most of the next month looked like. I called into my job the day she went into the hospital and said I would be out and honestly never thought about it again until I was asked when I was coming back. My heart was in a hospital bed, that job was not a priority at that moment. Neither was my growing business.

Before all of this I was working full-time, running a growing business, and raising a 10-year-old with my loving husband. I was also the friend that helped everyone, caring for my grandmother's needs and errands, a people pleaser, and an overachiever. This journey changed me in many ways. The first change was realizing what my priorities were. Most of the things that were so important prior to this really didn't seem to matter much. I honestly didn't care if I lost my job. Not in a malicious way, it just fell out of view. My main focus was taking care of my grandmother and maintaining normalcy for my son. Everything outside of those two, fell by the wayside.

After about a week in the hospital my grandmother started flexing her fingers in and out. I watched her do it over and over again and I finally asked her, "what are you doing?"

She replied, "if I can work my fingers, I can make my pies."

"Ma'am, you're in the hospital and you're thinking about making pies?"

It was a few weeks before Thanksgiving and she was so absolutely serious. Who thinks like that? You are not sure about your fate, but you are ready to go bake. I learned a lesson here too, but I didn't understand it until later. But she was serious. Over my childhood, she would make anywhere from 20-60 pies and give them out to neighbors, church members, family, and even the mail carrier! Everyone would be waiting for their pie the Wednesday before Thanksgiving. I secretly watched out her window as the neighbors would pretend to do yardwork just to make sure they were outside when she started handing out pies. She took it very seriously because food was how she expressed love. She would make the pies, and I would have to gift wrap them all. This tradition meant so much to her and even in her condition she held hope that she would be able to bake those pies again.

I continued to question her, still thinking the whole thing was absurd. She finally said, "I have three things I want to do before I leave here. I want to see Noah turn ten, get back to my house, and have another Thanksgiving."

My questions stopped after I realized that the *here* she was referring to was not the hospital. I wasn't ready to deal with her list. My son had already turned 10 and it all felt like a timer counting down to something I wasn't ready to face. I changed the subject, and we switched to joking about something else. The lesson that I learned much later was that in all situations you have to have hope and goals. Hope changes your view of even the worst situations. She had a reason to keep going and even if it seemed ridiculous to me, it was what mattered to her. Another lesson is to keep hold of what matters to you even if it doesn't make sense to anyone else.

She made it out of the hospital and back to her house despite the doctor's being uncertain if she would make it through the week.

She came home bedridden, but after being challenged by her hospice nurse to have coffee with her at the kitchen table, she was able to do so and was able to walk around the house with assistance.

She was more vibrant than she had been even before she had entered the hospital.

My Grandma was released on a no salt diet, which threw us a curve ball. She was the cook of the family, and she rarely ate anyone else's cooking. My husband made her some rosemary potatoes once that she liked. And his French toast. I was bestowed the honor of taking over the macaroni and cheese some years prior. There were a couple of other things that she enjoyed from others but not more than 10 things in total. So now this lady who only eats her own food and has high standards, has to eat a no salt diet. I took on the challenge because no one else was going to, and because a huge part of my heart needed to do it for her. Do you know how much salt there is in everything?

I had dabbled in this a little when my mother-in-law was on a low sodium diet, but this wasn't a couple of meals. This was all my Grandmother's daily meals along with all the ones for my household. I quickly found some favorites and an approved salt substitute but not without some back and forth. Apparently, crockpot turkey wings were too tender and taste different than the oven ones. Did I mention I was now back at work full-time? Yep, all the things. And it started feeling like *all* the things!

I started slipping away. It was weird because my Grandma had defied the odds and made it out of the hospital. She had more energy; she looked better and better every day. Meanwhile, I was slowly becoming a zombie. I was just going through the motions with no emotion.

Now I realized that I had never really had the time to process what had happened. My heart stopped when she got admitted to the hospital, but I just had to keep going. All that emotion was just bottled up and pushed away because I had things to do! Who has time to feel? Now all those feelings were resurfacing. I felt overwhelmed but I couldn't quite figure out why. My anxiety was through the roof because my Grandma had checked off two of the three things on her literal bucket list. Thanksgiving was like the grim reaper in my mind. As it approached, I became more and more nervous. But I just keep going like everything was normal.

I still remember vividly the moment it all began to crumble. I had come home from work and sank into the couch. I just wanted to sit down for a moment before I started on the dinners I had to cook, my family's and my grandma's for the next day. As I lay there, my body got heavier and heavier. When six o'clock hit, I could not bring myself to move. I told myself I would get up at six fifteen but still I could not move.

Every 15-minute increment passed, and I felt like cement on that couch. At seven, I heard my husband in the kitchen starting dinner. From then on it was hit or miss whether I could bring myself to do some of the most basic things. The house of cards had fallen, and I couldn't do anything but watch and pretend like it wasn't happening. I was smiling and interacting with others but inside I was falling apart. I didn't know what was happening or how to deal with it, but I knew that things had changed in a way that was different from anything that I had ever experienced. I would be "on" when I had to and then so completely "off" any other time.

Thanksgiving was approaching and the thought of it triggered so much fear. The day came, and it was so much like a normal Thanksgiving, but I was basically looking over my shoulder the whole time. My Grandmother made her pies and the family meal, with help from the family. I was excited for her but internally, I felt the final check of her to do list was ominous. That night I could not sleep. I have had too many of those late-night shatter your life calls in my life.

The night came and went. No call. I relaxed my immediate fear, but the gloomy cloud remained. I stopped feeling like death was looming, but I still was so empty. I enjoyed the time I spent with loved ones but not much else. I only felt anything when we were laughing or talking together. I was sinking deeper and deeper each day going through the motions with no feeling.

There were so many amazing things that I learned from my grandma, I also learned some things that are just straight trash. No better way to say it than that. I know that all lessons were in love and protection but that doesn't mean they are healthy. My Grandmother had buried half of her family prematurely. Her husband and three of her five children. My mom and her brother never made it to their forties. She carried it all with such strength. A few times, I saw her break but never in public and never for long. She was the rock through all things.

That was how I was raised. Just keep going no matter what. It sounds good on paper but in real life, bruh! When you are faced with losing a part of your heart, strong ain't it! But that is where I was, being strong, being composed, being the bigger person. Being everything but the puddle of emotions that were still shoved in that bottle. We laughed and talked about everything under the sun. One night, I finally got that eerie call that I almost forgotten was looming since my grandma had been doing so well. My cousin called and said I needed to get there and I immediately knew what he meant. I turned to the corner that I had turned a million times before but this time I was greeted with flashing lights and the crashing reality that she was gone. It is so weird how death takes the wind out of you no matter how much time you have had to process it. Even though she had been given a terminal diagnosis, she had bounced back so fiercely that it no longer felt eminent.

We enjoyed six more beautiful months beyond that terminal diagnosis in the hospital. And honestly, I was ok with her passing. Sad, of course, but I got six bonus months with her. She lived a life well done. What I was not prepared for was that I had lost myself.

In the months that followed, I was stuck in this space where I was not able to return to who I once was, but I also had not figured out how to move forward. It was like I was cemented on that sofa all over again. And just like before my husband was trying to help in any way possible but there was nothing he could do. I still can close my eyes and see that look of concern on his face as he repeatedly checked on me. In those sunken days, I realized that I had always been the support to others but had never allowed others to do the same for me. I was surrounded by people who loved me, but no one had experience with how to take care of me. And even worse, I had no idea either. I have heard so many times, "no one checks on the strong friend".

While that is true, this wasn't that. I had never allowed myself to be the weak friend, and no one had experience dealing with that version of me. That realization shifted something. I knew I had to figure out not only how to leave this place of sadness but also how to change the way I operated in my relationships. I slowly began to pick up the pieces of my life, but I was extremely careful not to pick up the pieces that I knew I didn't want back.

It is funny how reflecting on the life of someone you lost can inspire you so much. I wrote a tribute to my grandmother for her funeral program and the process released some of those feelings but also put some things into perspective. As I sat writing with tears flowing, I knew that there was a big hole in my world, but that she had filled me with so much in life that she would always be with me.

Even though she lived her life in the service of others, she also lived the life she wanted in the way that she wanted. She lived on her own terms so why was I doing what I was supposed to do instead of living how she did. She raised me to stand up for myself, but I was cowering to societal norms and expectations. I was living a life that looked good on the outside. It checked all the boxes, but it didn't feel as good on the inside. I was overwhelmed, burnt out, and unfulfilled. Her legacy gave me the strength to start making my desires non-negotiable. Also, there is something about losing someone with a great impact on your life that makes you bold in a different sort of way. If I can go on without someone that I could never imagine losing, then I can do anything else!

I knew I didn't want to be strong anymore, but I did want to be bold and committed to building the life that I actually wanted. Previously, I felt guilty for wanting more. I had a supportive husband, genius son, house, car, and job. Who was I to want more? But I finally remembered, I was the stubborn child that always made sure she got what she wanted. I was the granddaughter of a woman who would stand by herself in her beliefs and not have a single care what anyone else thought about it. I started to reflect on those life lessons that she had shared with me with a new set of lenses. Yes, she taught me strength, but she also taught me boldness. She taught me how to stay in line, but she also taught me how to speak my mind. It is my duty to carry her legacy with me as I build my own!

By the following year, my life looked so radically different. I left my job and bet on myself taking my business full-time. The things that I loved, my family, travel, and my now two businesses, became the center of my life. The cape came off! And went back on a few times. I still am in the service of others but no longer at the expense of myself. The best lesson I learned was balance. It was her gift to me. I can't remove service from my DNA; it is so deeply etched but I can be mindful of how it is incorporated into my life. My grandmother quite literally sacrificed her heart to make sure that everyone she loved was cared for. But I also know that she would not want that for me. Just like I don't want that for my son.

I renegotiated every part of my life and put the pieces back together in a way that made so much more sense. I started attaching my time to a cost. Sometimes financial and sometimes a debit from something that was more aligned with my desires. If I listen to my friend vent about the problem that she has had for years and taken zero steps to correct, then I will miss family time. If I undervalue my services and book up my time, I am robbing myself of the availability for a high-paying client. This was challenging because it required lots of moments of courage and confidence and a shift to the belief that my time was not free and it was valuable. I still work daily on remembering this and holding this boundary.

Another key was having long talks with God about what was next. I sat in so much silence until I had clarity. In the silence, it hit me! God is talking to us all the time, answering our questions and prayers, but our lives are so busy that we don't hear half of what it being said. One day, I was in conversation with God, and he was speaking so loudly and clearly that I said, "have you been talking at this volume this whole time or did you just get a new mic". I just kept creating quiet spaces to continue to hear His voice and move accordingly.

I went from going through the motions to creating fulfillment in my daily life. From working for someone else to running two businesses in areas that bring joy to myself and others. This shy kid is now a public speaker, coach, and the face of her business. I went from not having time for vacations to being asked "where are you now".

All because I learned to follow my heart!

SURVIVING THE ELDEST DAUGHTER SYNDROME BY BRIDGETT MCGILL

he eldest daughter syndrome is recognized as: the burden felt by the oldest daughter to serve as a form of third parent for her siblings, a role model to all family members, a caretaker for the home and even a support system for her parents.

"Bridge, wake your brother and sister up when Tom and Jerry goes off," my mother spoke through a loud whisper. "Okay Ma," I responded, stretched across the bed with my chin resting on the top of my stacked hands, watching the cartoon.

"I should be here by the time y'all get out of school." My mother gathered her purse and lunch bag and headed for the door, tapping my foot as she walked past, "See you later."

"Okay, bye Ma, see you later."

I watched the rest of the cartoon and began my daily routine of taking care of my siblings.

The eldest daughter syndrome looks different for every woman. In my case I was seven years old and in first grade when my syndrome began. After my mother and stepfather divorced, I instantly became responsible for my siblings. I had to pick up the slack, of what my stepfather was doing because he worked second shift. Since he was no longer around in the morning, this meant getting my three-year-old sister and five-year-old brother dressed before I put on my own clothes.

Luckily my sister was potty-trained, so I didn't have to worry about diapers or anything like that. My mother would make sure my sister had a change of clothes and everything she needed; I only had to get her to the sitter. My brother was a challenge at times, because he never wanted to end his worship of the cartoon gods. "I'm telling Ma if you don't come on," I would threaten and then turn off the tv. This was my last resort to get him to put on his shoes and grab his jacket.

We lived next door to the Fentry family. After we were dressed, we would lock the door, walk through the grass, taking my sister to the babysitter, and my brother and I would hold hands and walk across the street to Howe Elementary School under the watchful eye of the crossing guard.

School would end and I would pick up my brother from the front of the building and we would cross the street again, after some quick horseplay. Most times, if my mother didn't work over-time or get caught in some lengthy bus traffic, she would be at home and have already picked up my sister.

On the days she wasn't home, I would get the key and my sister from the neighbor, get all three of us in the house and snag an apple or orange – our favorite snacks, until my mother got home and started dinner. This was my life at seven years old.

When you're always responsible for somebody else, there aren't many times that you take a moment and think about yourself. You're always making sure that somebody else has their bus cards, everybody has their clothes out for the next day, or planning how we make the morning smoother.

Well, that was part of our nighttime routine. "You betta find those shoes you want to wear, because if you get up looking for them you ain't wearing them." I would fuss at my brother as we prepared for the next day."

"We betta not have to look for that jacket either."

This was our routine for a few years, how many, I can't exactly remember, but this is how my journey began. My mother would faithfully remind me to "Always take care of your brother and sister." This became the greatest part of my identity, their big sister.

My granddaughter is in first grade right now and I can't imagine her having that kind of responsibility.

As I was growing up, I always thought that I was cool as far as my existence because I didn't have the story of being raped or molested by family members or my mother's boyfriend. That idea was the furthest thing from the truth.

When you become "parentified' at a young age, your siblings forever view you as their big sister, best friend, confidant and their other mother. They depend on you for everything.

As adults, when they were about to move into an apartment they would ring me and say, "Hey, Bea, come check this apartment out before I sign the lease, and let me know what you think." If there was a situation with one of their children at school, I was called, "Hey, I can't leave work right now, can you run up to my daughter's school to see what's going on?"

Whenever my youngest sister got into any kind of trouble or made another trip to the police station, it was me who was called first.

Because I showed up for my siblings like this for most of my life, I developed a need to be needed and the spirit of co-dependency was born.

When I was a little girl, people would say, "She's so bossy", or "Here comes the boss." But nobody ever understood—that's how my mind worked because I was responsible for other people at such a young age.

I didn't view myself as a leader because I was always in survival mode. I didn't begin to see myself as a leader until I shifted into thrive mode.

That being said, I've never thought like a child. I have always thought: *What do we have to do? How do we get it done?* I don't start with "Oh, my God. What are we going to do?" I'm going to let you cry. I'm going to let you get all of the emotions out.

Then my next words will be, "Now let's make a move."

People have struggled to understand this part of me.

When people are discussing a problem, my mind is working: *What should they do? How do we fix that?* When people need to unload, I ask, "Hey, if you want me to just listen, or if you don't want a solution, and you just need to get all of this out, I need you to say that."

In many cases I've had to stand down. And I'm okay with people telling me, "Hey, right now, I just need an ear."

Every challenging situation that my siblings experienced; I was right there. "You need somewhere to stay? Okay. I'm going to put my kids in the bedroom with me and you and your kids take their bedroom."

One of my daughters had reached her breaking point of the forever revolving door to our home.

"Ma, you let people move in with you, but they move in on us, too. Me and Kayla didn't sign up for that."

It seems like a few years ago, but it was really more like a decade. Those words from my eldest daughter hit me like a ton of bricks. Her statement was the boulder thrown that put the crack in my formidable wall of "I gotchu", and initiated the healing that would eventually break down my thirty-five-year concrete wall of "Eldest Daughter Syndrome."

Every time my brother went to jail, I was on point, "Okay, what do we have to do? Put the money together so we can either bail him out or let's put some money on his books so he can be cool while he's in there."

My youngest sister, who was born when my other siblings and

I were 14, 12 and 10, was constantly getting into trouble when she was only 13. Dealing with her own demons and my mother's passing, presented its own set of challenges. Thanks to her, I have been to every police station in Chicago. I have been in project buildings where I brought the police with me because I walked into the station and told them "I need some help. My little sister is 14, she's on the 15th floor in the last building on Roosevelt." The police would accompany me to yank my sister out of an apartment where adults were doing some of everything and didn't care that she was ditching school or that she was underaged.

Most times, she would be hanging out in a project we called The Village—one of the most deadly and toxic complexes on the West Side of Chicago. On top of all this, my mother's drug addiction kicked in during my high school years. This shifted me into "Mama mode" for real. My responsibility for my siblings was geared into overdrive. My mother passing at the young age of 45 forced me into an advanced position of taking care of my family. I was 27 when we lost our mother and my sibling's father had already passed away. At the time, I barely had a relationship with my father. We were all we had. Despite all of those losses, there was nothing that was going to stop me from making sure my brother and sisters were all good—all the time.

Confidence or Worth?

IN 2020, at the beginning of COVID, during an early Saturday morning quiet time, I discovered something about myself that was life-changing.

I was sitting in my bedroom doing some journaling. I spoke my thoughts out loud. "I'm going to reduce the level of access that people have to me."

I thought about the bracelets on a jewelry store counter on

those circular stands. You know, the ones that everyone picks up and tries on and puts them back if they don't want them.

I'm not going to be like those bracelets. I'm not going to be that person anymore. I'm going to be the jewelry that's behind the case. The case the clerk needs a key to open.

This revelation began as a result of me finally making decisions to tell my family "No." As I thought about the jewelry in the case behind the counter versus the circular display, I considered the fact that those pieces of jewelry are valuable just sitting there in the case. They aren't doing anything. They are not adorning anyone's neck or wrist. They are just there and they are valuable. The light bulb came on.

Wait a minute. So, If I'm like the jewelry behind the counter, where no one has access to me, then that means that I'm valuable and worthy without doing anything for anyone? I'm simply valuable?

The Holy Spirit took over and brought clarity to my definitions of confidence and worth.

For all those years I found my value in taking care of my family. I confused confidence and my ability to lead in handling situations as my value. I had to just be still and hear the voice of the Lord.

You've been doing that since you were seven years old. You've always been a leader. You've always been a problem solver. You've always had confidence because that's just how you move. But if you never do another thing for anyone for the rest of your life, you my daughter are valuable.

That day, I sat in my chair and let the tears flow. I mean, I cried that ugly, snot wiping with the forearm kind of cry. I literally could see it. I was in my room wailing because I understood, finally, that worth and confidence was not the same thing.

And that's the thing with the eldest daughter. We base our worth on our works for other people. We determine our worth by performance. And we never understand until we shift. When we start pulling back and start saying, No! Then the toxic thoughts come through:

Well, what do I do now?
I'm not tending to my family.
I don't know everything that's going on with everyone.
Nobody's calling me for help.

The process didn't come easy. When I first started saying no, I would follow my response with all these explanations of *why* I couldn't do it. That instant guilt was doing all the talking. This left room for them to continue the conversation by trying anything and everything to persuade me.

Then I shifted into saying "No" with maybe just a little explanation. This was an attempt to make sure there was no wiggle room in the conversation for pressure or persuasion.

When I graduated to the *"No"* end of sentence, with a period or an exclamation point, that's when I began to feel empowered. It took many years to get to where I didn't feel the need to answer my family's every request.

My daughters were so tired of people living with us over the years, that we actually celebrated the first twelve months that nobody had moved into our space. At one point before I bought my house, I lived in a massive apartment with my two daughters, my middle sister, at least four of her six children, my youngest sister, her son and our brother.

We're pretty clean and we don't tear up things, but that was way too many people in one spot. This is what happens when the eldest daughter has not yet learned the importance of setting boundaries. My family needed somewhere to stay and I had a place for them. That's it and that's all.

As much as I thought I had protected my children, I was blinded by my loyalty to my family first and not my daughters' need for privacy and their own growth. I always had thoughts of:

I can't just let them be out with nowhere to go.
Where are they going to go?
They're going to go with somebody that's going to be mistreating them.

No, they're going to come with me.

I would solve a problem before it actually was a problem; even before they tried to figure it out on their own.

Unfortunately, it took me years to start protecting my children on a higher level and to start protecting myself. The healing was coming slowly but surely.

A second major stone was laid in my healing path about a year after my daughter told me how difficult it was for her with all the people in and out of our apartment. One niece was mad at her sisters so of course she wanted to spill some tea.

"Yeah Auntie, they've been talking about you bad. They've been saying you taking all day to let them know if they can have their parties at your house."

"Oh really, thanks for letting me know."

I confronted both of them and was met with apologies and "Naw, Auntie, it wasn't like that." I let them know in no uncertain terms that I wasn't feeling it or them.

"Y'all want to talk behind my back, and then use my house? Find someplace else."

And guess what, they did. And paid a nice little chunk of change for the venues. They certainly wouldn't have shelled out any dollars for me. Not that I would have asked, but still, it's the principal of it.

That was a major turning point for me with my family, because it became crystal clear, after sixteen years, that they didn't need me as much as I thought. They *were* able to figure out situations without me. I had just made myself so available, why would they do something different?

Healing Hurts

With healing comes revelation and growth. There are levels to healing and worthiness. The downside of spiritual downloads and revelations are the questions that surface in your subconscious.

If I know that I am worthy, what does my worthiness look like in other areas of my life?

For example, every time I sat behind the wheel of a new car, I would be scared to enjoy it. I didn't think that I was worthy of an upgrade. I didn't know this was in my subconscious thoughts. When I was set to receive a promotion at my job, I struggled with the new salary. I bought my house making a decent, but not hefty income.

I don't know. My boss might not do it. I hope she gives me that extra $15,000.

I had a whole degree, of course I was worthy. But I didn't feel that way.

And of course, in this segment we need to talk about the eldest daughter and relationships. I'm going to keep it brief, but I have to make the point of how this syndrome effects every area of your life.

When you have a need to be needed, you attract needy-ass people. You're going to always attract the man that needs your help with something. He may not need a place to live. He may not need your money, but he might need help with creating a resume, job searches, clearing his background, help with his children's education, etc.

He might need help reconnecting with his mother, family or his estranged children. He might need help with a payment for this or down payment on that. He might need help understanding his worth. Draining, draining, draining.

Honestly, all that other stuff was time-consuming. My internal thoughts would be

Here take this $150 and be gone, because I don't want to hear all that today.

A man who needs you and a man who wants you are two different men.

Let me say that again: A man who needs you and a man who wants you; those are two different men.

I never want another man who needs me. I only want the man who wants me because the man who wants me doesn't need anything from me. He wants encouragement. He wants me to respect and uplift him. Of course, he wants me to show him kindness and compassion, but he doesn't *need it*. If I don't give it to him, he's okay because he possesses what he needs within himself.

Being with a man who needs me means saying every day,

"You alright, King?"

"You doing good, Black Man?"

"I see you."

"I'm clapping for you today."

And none of that is ever poured back into you. And heaven forbid you miss a day; you're accused of acting funny or flipping the script. What?

A man that needs you, doesn't have the knowledge of his own worthiness. A man that wants you; he's well within himself. So, if you clap for him today and not tomorrow, he's still good because he's good internally.

Of course, like every man, encouragement and pouring into is important. Who doesn't want to be encouraged? But he isn't going to die if you don't give it to him. Again, these are two different men.

When men approach me now, with the "What are you looking for in a man" question, I have nothing. No list, no requirements. I know now that the man who chooses me, is choosing me because he's been watching me and understands a woman like me. What's the saying?

What's understood, don't need to be explained.

The man that's watching me is going to offer his assistance. He's going to ask what help do I need with upcoming events. He has a desire to make my life easier.

In the first book I wrote in 2017, I said there's three reasons a man chooses you.

One: He doesn't know his purpose, and he's just choosing you for carnal reasons.

Two: He knows his purpose, but he doesn't care about yours, instead he needs you to do everything to help fulfill his.

Three: He knows his purpose, and he's choosing you because he can see that your purpose is in alignment with his purpose.

Now that I have a more elevated view of myself, I don't even entertain men asking certain questions.

In my last relationship, we both had completely different perspectives of our relationship. We stopped pouring into each other and our season had ended. The eldest daughter syndrome wanted to fight for the relationship, but the elevated version of me said, "Nah Bea, let it be, there's something better. Don't hold onto what's dead; that effects your healing."

And I simply let go.

The HOW to the HEALING

Removing all thoughts and situations that no longer serve you, makes room for what's truly yours.

A huge aspect of the healing process is the how you heal. As the eldest daughter, a huge part of my healing process was going back to the little girl Bridgett and the teenager Bridgett. I had to go back and have some conversations with them and make some apologies and give both of them some reassurances that in due time, we were going to be okay.

I had to tell little girl Bridgett that it wasn't her fault that she was "parentified" at seven years old and that later in life, she was going to be doing well. I had to tell teenager Bridgett that she wasn't going to always be in survival mode, and she would be able to exhale, when she entered her thrive phase of life.

I had to tell the thirty-something year old Bridgett that you don't have to give away everything and it's okay to let other people figure out their own lives.

The most beautiful aspect of healing is that opportunities will come looking for you, because you are finally ready to receive them.

People are suddenly referring you and dropping your name in amazing spaces. People are saying things about you and you aren't even in the room. Why? Because you've made space to receive.

Those opportunities become gifts rather than challenges. When we are unhealed, we view these sudden chances as burdens, and respond to an offer with "No Sis, I'm going to pass. I can't add one more thing to my plate."

With healing, we view that same opportunity as a vehicle to help someone as well as ourselves.

Clear the plate. That way your plate is now open to receive universal gifts, such as being part of an anthology like this one.

I thank God, because healing opened doors that I may not have been ready for. Opportunities came that I may have not been able to receive had I still been in this dynamic of

I have to do everything for my family. I've got to help them with this. I got to help them with that.

In healing, I made room for growth *and* spaces and places. I made room for me.

Since 2020, I've done a lot in my community and in the literary arena, because room was made.

I'm now more discerning with how I spend money, offer help and lend my resources. I've learned in real time that a taker will keep taking and a giver will keep giving. The distinction must be discerned.

The Difference

One final aspect I want to mention is the difference in the eldest daughter syndrome and the eldest son syndrome.

Eldest daughters take on much more naturally than eldest sons because girls are natural nurturers. The oldest boy is taught to take care of his siblings from the protector aspect. But the dynamic is different and so are the conversations.

The big brother is going to say "Let's go, Joe." "Ain't no crying, Let's go."

It's not like that with the girls because we're going to help you up. We're going to pat you on the back. We're going to snuggle and tell you 'We still have to get this thing done.'

The eldest boys have mindsets of soldiers.

"Man, suck that up. We got to get sh*@ done."

The glaring difference is the eldest son is positioned to protect his siblings because legacy lasts more than one day. For men, protecting the family name and image is a huge part of their identity. The role model aspect is important; he knows that his siblings are watching every positive and negative thing he does.

"That's not how we get down", is a familiar statement from the eldest son to his siblings as a form of guarding the family name.

The eldest daughter syndrome has us treating everyone like our own baby.

"I know my baby needs me. I know my family needs me."

We have to be careful of falling into that codependency; because we don't think there's anything wrong with it.

Let's be clear, this syndrome is not determined by family dynamic. This birth position syndrome is not characterized because of a single parent or two parent household; it's simply the plight of the eldest child.

. . .

THE COST

IN CLOSING, I want to share about a few loses I've suffered living in this state of mind.

One Christmas one of my sisters wanted to buy her daughters some boots as a gift.

All my bills were paid and there was nothing left to spare, so I took out a payday loan that had some interest attached to it. When it was time to pay the money back, she gave me the initial money and I asked, "Okay, what's up with the interest?"

"The agreement wasn't for the interest." She said with no fumbling or stumbling.

You thought I would have learned, but I wasn't quite there yet.

That same sister went to jail and needed $500 to get out. Her kids called me in a panic. "Auntie, our mama in the county jail, we need $500 to get her out." Because of some past money situations, that created a loss for me, I had limitations with cash.

This time, my boundary spoke for me, "I got $200."

My niece replied, "Well, how are we going to get the rest?"

"I don't know. But I got $200."

A year went by. Another year went by without any acknowledgement of repaying the loan.

When I asked, "When are you going to give me my money?"

She'd reply, "Oh, I'm going to give it to you. I ain't got no expected date."

I guess she was tired of me asking her and finally said, "You know what? You can stop asking me for that money."

She said it with her whole chest.

"Just like other people didn't pay you back, I ain't paying you back either."

Straight like that. No chaser, no nothing.

I said, "You know what? I'm not even mad at you because now I know, and I'm glad you finally said it so that I could stop asking you about the money, but now I know."

What that situation did was close the door on anything ever having to do with money between us. She's still my sister, and I love her always.

"It's cool."

I should have learned my lesson from the boot incident, but I didn't. But trust me, my new boundary heard it loud and clear. In years past I would help her with each of her children during prom time. Her grandchildren are starting to go to prom, I'm showing up for the support but that's it. No help with shoes, dresses, corsages, fees or anything else.

I once put a car in my name for my brother because he needed a car to move around in. Unfortunately, he let his friend drive the car, who ended up in an accident. I was sued by the vehicle owner for $8,000. Yes, my brother paid every dime of the money, but I ended up going back and forth to court three times. And I was by myself each time. Neither he nor the driver showed up for any court dates.

Even so, I hadn't gotten the full lesson. A guy I dated some years back asked if I could put his car in my name for thirty days, just to get the car off the lot. Well in those thirty days, this dude got $1,000 in tickets. By the time those tickets doubled, I owed $2,000 to the city. Did he give me a dime? He did not. But this was supposed to be my man.

"Look just give me the plates off the car and I'm good," I told him

"What am I supposed to do about plates?" he asked.

"I don't know, but you keep getting these tickets and that's effecting me."

I went into my West Side upbringing.

Tonight is the last night this trick is gonna get a ticket in my name.

I borrowed a friend's car and went to get my "always up for some drama" little sister. "Okay look. Go in the bar and tell K.T. I said come here. When you come out, don't come towards the car in case he comes out behind you. I'm gonna spin the block and grab you."

"Okay Sis, bet."

I turned off the lights and engine and watched from across the street.

K.T came out looking up and down the street for me and my sister.

Now spooked. He got in his car and took off. I started the car, and crossed the intersection, and motioned for my sister to get in the car. Pulling up to the house I went into stealth mode.

I had on gym shoes, but when I stepped from the car, I was like a Ninja with a Phillips screwdriver in my hand.

"Watch the gangway. If you see him, blow the horn." I told my sister.

"Alright girl, hurry up, you know I'm on papers." Meaning, she was on probation.

"Just watch my back, we're good."

I bent down in the front of the car, and gently removed the front plate. Taking periodic peeks over the hood towards his building.

I stooped to get the back plate and pressed too hard, setting off the alarm.

"Dammit." Before I could get the plate off, K.T. came running from his gangway.

"Gurl, what are you doing?" he yelled and tried to snatch the plate from my hand.

Jerking back from him, I stood as tall as my 5'5" would let me against his 6'2".

"I told you to stop getting tickets in my name." When he tried to snatch the plate again, it cut my hand.

"Now look, I wasn't even trying to do that. Come on man, we ain't gotta do this. I'll bring the plates tomorrow."

My brother had a reputation that preceded him. He had voiced on many occasions, "Man, I've been waiting a long time to beat somebody up about you Sis."

"You don't have to call your brother or your people, I'll bring you the plates tomorrow."

"No, you gonna give me the plates right now."

People began to come outside and be nosey. I got in the borrowed car and left

before the situation got any uglier. An hour later, I heard a sound at my steel gate. It was K.T. putting the plates between the poles at the top of the fence.

Now, you can't get me to put anything in my name for anyone.

After one heated debate with my younger sister, she said matter-of-factly. "I don't be asking you for nothing, you be offering." Well, well, well, she had just turned on another healing lightbulb for me. I forever thank her for saying this. It didn't work out too good for her after that, but it did need to be said—out loud. I can go on and on about my losses, but I think you get the picture.

When my family comes to me with a situation, rather than offer assistance, I only offer to help them work through the situation.

I no longer offer any help, financially or otherwise. If I hand over any money it's with the thought of 'I don't need it back'. I release it and let it go.

The eldest daughter syndrome comes with toxic relationships and losses. But you don't have to be stuck with the consequences of this syndrome, it comes with healing if you put in the work.

Healing is such a beautiful space to be in. Healing isn't just for those who are sick in the moment, healing can also keep someone from becoming sick, you know like preventative medicine. As I continue to share my story through various platforms, there will be another teenager, young adult or thirty-something woman, that will learn the importance of setting boundaries, taking care of herself and/or her family and letting others take care of themselves. She will learn that it's okay to not step in, and she doesn't have to rush in to save the day. In fact, the people around us really can take care of and figure things out for themselves. I pray she learns these lessons a lot earlier than I did.

Yes indeed, I am healed from the Eldest Daughter Syndrome.

EMBERS RISE: I'M NOT SUPPOSED TO BE HERE BY YVONNE ELLIOTT

*"*A*lways remember that striving and struggle come before success in the dictionary."* —Sarah Ban Breathnach

I DIDN'T REALIZE it when I was born, but I have angels watching over me. My first angel stepped in when I was born. Weighing 2.5 pounds at St. Luke Presbyterian hospital in 1980, that I even survived birth is a miracle. I've listened to my grandmother and godmother tell the story many times. The storytelling began at family gatherings, as sunlight, cocoa butter, and barbeque perfumed the air.

Aluminum foil pans of potato and macaroni salad joined the bottomless bowls of chips and pretzels on one end of the table. Cake stands filled with all kinds of desert lined another. The faint smell of freshly cut pineapple wafted in the air, indicative of the prized hand-churned pineapple sherbet that ended every family function. Kids my age and older hovered around that table, sneaking fingersfuls of icing before running off to continue a game of freeze tag or another dance contest, all under the watchful eyes of their mothers. I'd walk up, hug, and say hello to my godmother, and she'd respond with the same thing each time.

"You're a pretty little girl," she said, while shooting a knowing look at my grandmother.

My grandmother often chimed in with, "Yes, she is."

Then my godmother would say. "We weren't always sure how you'd look. When you were first born, you looked like a little rat."

My eyes always lowered when she said that. All I could picture were the little newborn rats I'd seen in science books in the library. Then my grandmother would interject. "Yes, you looked like a little rat when you first came out. You didn't have any hair, no eyelashes, nothing. Only a tiny body with a heartbeat and a brain.

"Yeah, like a bald little rat," my godmother said with a chuckle.

"But suddenly…" my grandmother's voice turned sweet. That change in tone was my godmother's cue to nod and agree.

"It's like God took a pencil and started to draw."

"Um-hum," they'd said together.

"Each day, I traveled to the hospital to visit you, and each time, it was a new experience." My grandmother said, "One day you didn't have eyelashes, then I came back, and you had eyelashes. One day no eyebrows, then the next day, eyebrows. Suddenly, there was your beautiful little brown face."

She'd turn to look at me and smile before my godmother chimed in.

"Yeah, the nurses called you 'Chocolate Drop'."

Then they hugged me, patted me on the behind, and sent me on my way. Somehow, a micro-preemie born in 1980 survived, but my initial struggles set the stage for many challenges in my life. Fear for me never came in the guise of a vampire or werewolf or giant, as one would find in children's books. Part of me would have welcomed the imaginary one. The real ones made you cry. The human ones made you scream.

Someone broke into our apartment on Lawndale Avenue in

Chicago when I was five. With nothing but the clothes on our backs, my mother packed us up and flew us to California. As my mother worked through her issues, we were like nomads, for a few months moving from one place to another. I found out later her 'grown up' problems began and ended with an addiction.

Another angel swept into my life a few years later on the day a drug dealer severely beat my mother. Since I wasn't old enough to be left home alone during the day, Mom took me with her when she went to score drugs. That day, she sent me to the taco truck with three dollars to get some rolled tacos, a cheap, quick meal. I waited in front of the liquor store, just as my mother had instructed.

It's always there in the back of a child's mind when a parent is late coming to pick them up. Sometimes it creeps in like a nagging feeling. After it happens three or four times, it settles over you like a soggy cloak.

She forgot where she left me. I must have forgotten to clean up my toys, or maybe I was too loud, and she got so mad that she just left me behind and...and...

Terrifying images built in my head as I craned my neck to see where she had gone. That same wild fear made my heart cramp in my chest as I hurried down the street in the direction she went.

I wasn't a baby anymore. Babies cried. Little girls whined and wiped their noses on their shirtsleeves.

By the time I reached the end of the parking lot, I was in a dead run. She wasn't there. My heart rattled against my ribcage as reality set in. And then, a familiar blue sports car pulled up next to me. The vehicle belonged to a man my mother had befriended.

"Get inside," he barked through the rolled-down window before shoving the front passenger side door open.

I started walking towards the car, then froze. My mother's words rang in my head.

Don't talk to strangers, and whatever you do, never get into someone's car, — even if you know them, — without them knowing our secret password.

"Where's my mom?" I asked, backing away from the car.

"She's in the mobile home up the street. "Now come on," he snapped. I looked toward where he was pointing and there was my mom, covering her face with a shirt.

"Yonne, get in the car with Lars," she ordered before staggering to the mobile home a few feet away.

"No, I want to go with you," I called as I took a few steps in her direction.

"No, get in the car with Lars. Do as I say. He's going to take you home," she said, wincing as a stranger helped her into the back of the vehicle.

By then, I was crying. "Where are you going?" I whined, not knowing what was going on or what happened.

Lars guided me into the front seat of his car, and we followed the mobile home as it pulled out onto the main road. Through the back window of the mobile home, I could see my mother rocking back and forth, still holding that bloody shirt up to her face. We followed the mobile home until we hit the expressway. We turned, but the mobile home continued straight.

"She'll be okay, Yonne. Let's get you home to bed," he said, trying hard to keep the smile in his voice, but all I had to do was close my eyes, and my mother, covered in blood, filled my mind.

Lars took me back to the apartment we shared with him. He put me in bed and told me my mother would be all right. When I am scared, I would rock myself to sleep and say a little chant in my head: I'm cold, I'm hungry, and I want my mommy, I'm cold, I'm hungry, and I want my mommy.

As I chanted, the words swirled within me, circling the gaping hole in my heart where my mother should have been. The harder I cried, the more the chant morphed and grew louder than my tears, and my heartbeat began thumping in my ears as the words swelled in my throat.

I want my mommy, and then I want my granny. I want my granny; I want my granny.

A dream unfolded: God scooped me up, flew me to Chicago, and placed me safely in my grandmother's familiar, warm bed. I don't know how it happened, but my angel came and got me. The next thing I remember, I was in my grandmother's bed.

Many years later, in my late 30s, I shared the story with my aunt as we piled into my car for a day of running errands. She had the strangest look on her face as tears gathered in her eyes.

"That was me," she said finally before shifting her focus to the safety of the rushing traffic.

"Huh?" I asked as I quickly divided my attention between driving the car and watching her stumble over the memories.

"Yonne, that was me; I was the one that came and got you, she said, wincing at some private thought. "We were in the basement doing hair when the phone rang. Your grandmother spilled into the chair with this look on her face. "We got to go get Yonne," she said. "Something happened to Nire, and we got to go get Yonne." My aunt looked at me with tears leaking from the corners of her eyes.

"Baby, Granny, hung up that phone, went upstairs to her room, and came out with some cash. I threw some clothes in a bag and was on my way to the airport on the next flight out to get you."

My eyes welled up with tears. "It was you? You're my angel?" My voice cracked with emotion. "I swear, Tee, I remember nothing that happened from when I was in Lar's car. I don't know how I got back to Chicago or how much time had passed."

When we got to our destination, as soon as we got out of the car, I walked over to my aunt and wrapped my arms around her. Hugging her tightly. I whispered in her ear, "Thank you for saving me."

How could I know other angels would appear to shelter me from the coming storms in the years to come?

One person's actions can change another's entire life. Looking back, I see certain people who showed up when I needed them most—people who taught me faith and became invaluable to me. I call them angels because they appeared and made a way when there seemed to be no other option. Like pebbles dropped into a lake, their small actions created ripples that changed everything around them, even though they might not have realized their impact.

Faith became an essential tool. The Bible describes faith as

the substance of things hoped for, and the evidence of things not seen.

My angels appear just when my confidence is running low or has disappeared. Through their presence, I learned to strengthen what I call my faith muscles. Even when things don't turn out as I'd hoped, I now understand that everything happens for a reason, and when I need help, an angel is never far away.

Rebirth Activity: Look back at your life and identify any angels that have shown up for you. If they are still alive, call them and tell them how they were the angel in your life.

Memories
"I hate getting flashbacks of things I don't want to remember." - Unknown

Addiction is the only disease I know where feeding the darkness satisfies the addict, but it starves the people around them. I know what a crack pipe looks like—glass with cotton inside, drugs burned on top. I know the smell: burning plastic mixed with hot metal. Thirty-plus years later, I can still identify that scent, whether it's mixed with weed, incense, perfume, or sex. I learned that smell at age seven. It's burned into my memory, and like a bullet, it shoots me back to when I was young and vulnerable.

After relocating to California, we moved into an apartment

complex right up the street from where my auntie lived. It was a two-bedroom, and I had my own room, just like when we were at home in Chicago. My mother befriended a woman who lived in the complex. She had two daughters. One was my age, and her sister was a teenager. They lived in a two-story townhouse. It was the first time I'd ever seen a townhouse, and when we first visited, I had fun running up and down the stairs. The girls shared a room, and the younger girl had tons of Barbie dolls and a dream house. I thought it was so cool since I left most of my toys in Chicago.

One evening, my mom told me we were going over to their house for a while. I was excited to play with other kids because I'd spent much of my time playing alone. The girl my age and I played with her Barbie dolls, but it got late, and I wanted to go home, so I headed downstairs and told my mom. She was busy drinking beer and smoking cigarettes. She waved me away and sent me back upstairs.

After a time, the girl's mom came up and told us to get ready for bed. I didn't have any pajamas, so she told her daughter to give me some; she did, and I changed clothes and got on the bed to go to sleep, but the younger girl started kicking me and saying mean things. I started crying and decided that I was ready to go home.

I left the bed and walked towards the bedroom door to search for my mom. Upon opening it, a burning odor hit my nose. Music blared; smoke filled the air. As I moved further down the stairs, I could hear popping and crackling sounds, sharp inhalations, and adults talking in raspy voices.

I crept down one stair, and I called, "Mom."

Continuing down the stairs, I called again. My eyes burning from the thickening smoke. As I peeked around the corner, I noticed my mom putting a pipe to her lips.

This time, I shouted, "Mom!"

Her eyes widened as she looked at me. Her friend then noticed me and a gasp broke the silence in the room as my mom, coughing, pulled the pipe from her mouth.

She yelled, "Yonne! Go back upstairs!"

I tried to go back the way that I came, but it felt like my feet were stuck to the floor.

I put my face in my hands, and I started to cry.

"No!" I said. "The girls are mean to me."

She rushed to the stairs. "We're almost ready to go home, just a little while longer," she said

"But Mom, they are mean to me; I can't sleep."

"Okay, baby, I'll talk to them." She walked me back up the stairs and told the girls to be nice to me so we could go to sleep.

As my mom closed the door, the older girl tossed a pillow at my head, jeering, "Here, blackie, you can sleep on the floor like a dog!"

I thought about going back downstairs, but I feared what I might see. So, I did what I thought was the lesser of the two evils. I took the pillow and laid it on the cold tile floor. I curled up into a ball and tried to fall asleep, but it was cold, and I didn't have a blanket.

I closed my eyes and imagined I was home in Chicago, in my grandmother's bed. I chanted, *I want my granny, I want my granny, I want my granny and* rocked myself to sleep on the floor. A while later, my mom woke me up and took me home. Once we got there, I told her what the girls had done to me and told my mom I didn't want to play with them anymore.

A few months later, my mother stopped talking to her friend, and we moved to another apartment. Even though I never saw that family again, the memory of my mom with a crack pipe never left me. That was when I first connected the dots and understood why my mom slept during the day and stayed up all night. I didn't know what she was smoking, but I knew she acted differently and not like herself. That was the first time I felt alone and afraid; my idea of safety and security was destroyed. I didn't trust her to take care of me, and I realized I needed to figure some things out on my own.

This might not be the most helpful advice in the world, but the one thing that helped me the most was compartmentalization. Experts might say it's unhealthy but at the time it was all I had and as a result as I got older, I got good at placing things into mental boxes in my brain, and I'd gaslight myself into thinking that what I saw wasn't real. Sometimes, if you squint hard enough, you can almost see what should've been instead. Unfortunately, even the best memories fray at the edges, and when seen through the eyes of a child, the edges rarely matter.

Sometimes the memories come back, but I've gotten good at not trying to put them back in. I examine them like a fine piece of china, and if it doesn't serve me anymore, I let it go, and I fill that box with other things. I made space for joy, love, and hope. As a result, I'm pretty optimistic. The memories come from time to time, but when they do, there's no space for them, so they're unable to take over my brain.

Rebirth Question: What do you do with your memories when they come up? I encourage you to let them rise to the surface and journal about them.

Getting Help

"Be strong enough to stand alone, smart enough to know when you need help, and brave enough to ask for it." —Ziad K. Abdelnour

The first time I remember getting 'help' to deal with my mother's addiction, I was eleven or twelve years old. I was living with my grandmother in Chicago by then and had recently learned that my father had gotten married and I also learned that he had other children. One summer, my stepmother who was a psychologist and recovering addict herself—decided we were old enough to attend the annual Alcoholics Anonymous Founders Day conference in Akron, Ohio. She piled me, my two half-sisters, and my young niece into the car for the six-hour drive.

In the car, she said, "You're going to attend the Al-Anon meetings."

I did not know what that was or why I needed to go, but it wasn't Chicago, and my mom wasn't around, so I didn't argue.

In one weekend, I learned what an Al-Anon was, what an enabler was, and what I could do as a kid to deal with a parent who was on drugs. They told us it wasn't our fault, that abuse of a controlled substance is an illness and that our parents were sick, but they could only get better if they wanted to. Back then, I didn't know if I believed all the dogma they preached, but I discovered other kids out there like me; I wasn't alone.

Until that point, no one talked about what my mom did or explained that she was on drugs and how it affected me. My family didn't openly talk about her issues. It was like having a bull in a china shop run around and break all the items. The owners just cleaned up the broken pieces, put new china back on the shelf, and opened business the next day, hoping no one noticed. Even though the bull got put out of the shop every few days, it would come back. Everyone knew it was the bull, but nobody said anything to stop it from coming into the shop out of fear of upsetting the bull even more. Everyone just tried to pray the anger out of the bull.

That weekend let me know I wasn't crazy. Sadly, I realized my actions would not make my mother stop doing drugs. She would have to hit rock bottom to climb back up and my entire family and I were along for the ride.

I was twenty, the second time I remember getting 'help' with my mommy situation. I'd joined the AirForce and lived away from my mother. They stationed me in Maryland, and I was living my best life in my apartment. I needed to take a test to become proficient at my new job. It required me to study hard on my own time while learning the hands-on portion at work.

I couldn't study during the workday, so I needed to study before or after working a twelve-hour shift. When I took the test, I scored 63%, and I needed 65% to pass. I was devastated and had frequent panic attacks. I tried to deal with the panic attacks on my own, but they got so bad it made it hard for me to leave my apartment—especially during harsh weather.

One rainy day, I had to run an errand. While I was driving, the weather got worse, and I started hyperventilating. I pulled over so I wouldn't get into an accident. After a few minutes, I pulled myself together well enough to drive back home. I never got to where I was going; that's when I decided I needed to get help.

Initially, I felt like there was no one I could trust until I realized I had a trained psychologist right in my family. My stepmother was a counselor who kept other people's thoughts and helped them through difficult times. If she could do that for others, maybe she could do the same for me.

I found courage through my first love—writing. Even though finding the exact words was difficult, typing them out gave me the outlet I needed to ask for help. I sent her an email sharing how I was feeling and what was going on in my life.

She responded without judgment or shame; she understood what I was going through and offered suggestions to help me. I was also made to promise her I would see someone in person. She offered me a life raft and gave me the courage I needed to call a therapist and start my journey towards getting the help I needed.

I went to see my first therapist and explained my experience in the car, and she asked me if anything significant had just happened. I told her about the course failure and that I feared being kicked out of the military and that the fear of having to return home consumed me. By working with the counselor, I learned that my biggest fear was that my course failure would turn me into a crack head. She wanted to put me on an anti-anxiety medication, but I refused. Instead, we had six months of intense weekly sessions. It was enough to clear my mind and help me realize what I could and couldn't control. I could understand that the failure of a course didn't equate to failing in life.

While attending therapy, I wanted to go home on vacation, but the thought of going back crippled me. I was conflicted between wanting to visit my family and friends but not wanting to see my mother. I told the therapist that my mother was like a tornado. One day during my session, I told my therapist, "I feel like she sucks the air out of a room."

Throughout my sessions, as I cried in the oversized chair, she taught me how to put on a "gas mask" to go home, visit my family, and make it out alive. I expressed my fears about my visit. We went over what to do if my mother asked me for money and how to make sure my possessions didn't get stolen. I made it through my visit and helped me overcome that huge obstacle in my life. I passed the test on my second try and remained in the AirForce. That first therapist taught me about boundaries. I learned why I needed boundaries with my mother and how to set them with her and the people that I cared about.

In my mind, I was "cured". I could put on my pretend gas mask and move forward with life. But things were not as cut and dry as they seemed. So, I prayed… prayed as I struggled through the panic attacks. When I felt prayer wasn't working, sleep and books became my two best friends. Dreaming of worlds, I longed to be a part of instead of my current reality. Thinking I could sleep and wake up as one of the heroes in the tales I consumed, only to open my eyes the next day, realizing everything was the same. Those are the cues that let me know that I still need to ask for help from time to time. I call them my mental health tune ups.

Some of my therapy stints only last a few months, others a few years. When I find my inner child rising, that's my sign that it's time to go back to the couch, to find the source of what's bothering me. To learn about new tools and maybe refresh myself on some old ones, and to check on the little girl inside of me. She's still there, reminding me of joy and my purpose. But even she needs to be reminded that she is safe, she is loved, she is protected, and she is beautiful. Seeking help gives me the perspective I need when I've forgotten or lost my way. Growth and progress are not linear, nor is it a set it and forget it. It's okay to talk about your trauma no matter its depth, you are not alone and the sooner you realize a lot of us have a shared lived experience the faster we can break the chains we didn't ask for and seek the healing and emotional growth we deserve.

Rebirth Action: I encourage you to talk to a certified therapist and no, your family and friends aren't enough. It's time for you to experience your own rebirth. My story can also be yours. Will you start your journey towards experiencing your own rebirth?

BREAKING FREE BY CATHY A. BROWN

No punches were thrown, but still, bruises were left. I was held captive, imprisoned by the weight of guilt that didn't belong to me, brought on by the manipulation and abuse. Emotional abuse and gaslighting constructed the bars of my cell. I asked myself numerous times why I married him. I married because I felt we could create a family of our own. We married because we both wanted a sense of security. When I take the time to reflect on the whole experience, I can't help but feel there were some individuals who preferred that I stay a captive. Because that's just what women do. We stay sometimes regardless of the outcome. Hello, my name is Cathy and I stayed in a marriage despite the damage it was doing to my mental health.

The heartache from a previous break-up made me feel I needed to do something different. We met online at the start of the online dating era and became friends before pursuing a romantic relationship. He met my friends who were receptive to him, but in the back of my mind I felt something was off. He didn't fit into our circle, but he wasn't their friend, so this didn't matter much to me. When Peter first attended my church, he was invited by a friend of mine. Our church had encouraged us to invite a visitor, and my friend asked him before I could. He eventually joined and got involved in the ministry. It felt good to be on the same page spiritually with the person I loved. While we dated, Peter was attentive to my wants and desires. If I mentioned liking something I saw on a commercial or expressed an interest in a particular trinket, he would surprise me with it. He was thoughtful during this time and did things to bring me joy. When I said I do, it was out of pure love. I was excited about our future together and had great hopes of where it would go. I thought he was my one true love, but it turned out I wasn't going have my fairy tell ending.

For the sake of privacy, I will refer to my Ex as Peter. Just evidence again of the ongoing need to try to look out for him, one of the complications of being an empath. Being able to be concerned for the well-being of others is a great character trait. However, when you have someone used to being a receiver, they will continue to take as long as you are giving. That's what life with Peter was like for me. Once I care about you, I care. Out of my love for him, I protected him and made sure his needs were taken care of. Peter experienced chronic kidney disease the majority of his life. It required him to complete dialysis three times a week up to four hours per treatment. I genuinely wanted to be an additional support to him. I loved Peter and he loved me; our marriage was far from being loveless in the beginning. But when the goal of your partner is to always be one step ahead of you, it causes you to wonder *do they love me for me or what I can do for them?*

When it came time to let my family know I was ending my marriage, I was concerned they might mistake my decision for a reaction to grief. My mother had passed away about three months before, so my feelings were still pretty raw. She also lived with us for several years before her death. Her presence in our home wasn't a factor when it came to the problems within our marriage; the issues were already present before her arrival.

Making a big decision so soon after such a loss might be seen as irrational. However, my family was extremely supportive since they saw the red flags I wasn't willing to acknowledge from the beginning. They were able to see the bigger picture because they weren't blinded by love. When family members would bring his actions to my attention, I would always excuse it by saying, "That's just him," or "that's just the way he is". When I finally told them I was leaving him, they knew I had reached my limit. My family knows that once Cathy is done with something and her mind is made up, there's no turning back.

There were some moments I questioned if I was making the right decision for me. I remember when my sister asked, "You know it's okay for you to change your mind?" That never crossed my mind as being an option. I've always taken the mindset that if I commit to something, I have to walk it all the way through. Tweaking a decision here and there to make it work was one thing but to completely say I don't want to do it had never been an option for me. From career goals to friendships, I always stuck with my choices. Marrying this man was a covenant with God saying, 'til death do us part.' I told myself "Girl, you're just going to have to suck it up because this is who you chose to marry". With that in mind, I did the best I could to make this a successful marriage. Until I couldn't do it anymore.

Was the marriage one sided? Well, it definitely wasn't equal because a double standard existed in our marriage. Certain levels of transparency were expected of me that were not required of Peter. He had a desire to track my every move and didn't want me out of the home late if I wasn't doing something for him. This was not acceptable to me. At first, it was under the guise of, "I just need to know that you're safe. I need to know that you're okay." Actually, it was more of, "Well, as long as I can put my finger on her, I can have some say and control over what is happening." This was triggering for me since I observed my mom go through the same thing. My dad once put a tape recorder in my mom's car hoping to catch her talking with someone else. Peter once used a baby monitor to record my phone conversation. I felt like I was walking in my mother's shoes.

We entered our marriage knowing that I was going to make more money than him. I was just beginning my career as a mental health therapist, and he worked various jobs with a desire to complete his Bachelor's degree in Information Systems one day. At the age of twenty-six, I was clueless about what it would mean to be the primary earner for a household. At first, I looked at it no different than when I was single. I just had to purchase more food, toiletries and household items. No big deal, right? Boy was I wrong! The weight of making sure bills got paid, food was in the house, things for everyday living, all fell on me. Peter didn't like the way I did laundry and he knew it was a dreadful chore for me. Him doing laundry made everything else bearable. Unfortunately, it doesn't take much to please me.

When we first met, he was working part-time while receiving disability. He was able to care for himself prior to us getting married but didn't understand what it would mean to be a provider of someone other than himself. Eight months before we got married, he received his third kidney transplant and he was able to retain his disability and insurance. The disability and insurance coverage ended as soon as we said "I do" and we needed the income to cover his anti-rejection medications.

He went through a major period of quitting jobs. If it was something he wasn't really interested in or if he felt it didn't accommodate what he wanted to do, he would just quit. I came home on my lunch break one day because I forgot something. And who was home chilling when they should have been at work? You guessed it! He never talked with me about making the decision to quit, I was expected to be okay with his choice and keep the household running as usual. Another time he was with a temporary agency working production either second or third shift. He didn't like it and told me, "I don't know if I can do this." I told him "You're going to have to figure it out." As an adult, I couldn't tell this grown man what to do. We both knew we had bills to pay. Well, he figured it out, he left the job. We were behind on bills and in debt to the point where my car got repossessed. When we had the conversation about our finances, he said, "Why didn't you tell me?" I'm thinking, "Negro, you live here, too!" Peter could have made himself more aware of what was going on if he wanted to. Even with that, he made it *my* fault because I didn't bring it *to his* attention. In hindsight, this was one of the first incidents of gaslighting I experienced.

Fourteen years into our marriage was the first time I considered we weren't going to make it to forever. I remember saying to a family member "I don't know if I can continue on with this marriage". Peter and I were married in two thousand and four. The first seven years we dealt with his inability to maintain employment, financial stressors, and my lack of trust in his ability to keep his word. During this time Peter was in school to finish his degree. He was enrolled to take a class during the summer session and we agreed that he wasn't going to work so he could focus on his studies. Summer sessions are shorter than a regular semester and jam packed with assignments, so it made sense to honor this request. Peter was taking a Physics class that was very difficult. He dropped the class without discussing it with me. While I thought he was in class or at school studying he was reneging on his word. When I confronted him about this, he told me I wasn't supportive and I didn't understand the pressure he was facing being a nontraditional student. I was also told that I should have put in more effort to help him with his assignments. I reminded him how I was able to work full time and go to school to finish my Master's degree in counseling during the early years of our marriage. This fact didn't matter; he told me "Anyone could do what I went to school for." He didn't want to be held accountable and he talked down about the field that was keeping a roof over our head. Peter was a quick thinker and would find a way to point the finger at me.

When it came to making the church aware of the issues in my marriage, I was hesitant. This was the church I had been a member of since college. It was so different from the traditional views of church that I grew up in because the Pastor was a woman. Growing up, women could be an Evangelist but to have one leading a church and behind the pulpit every Sunday wasn't the norm. Being under the leadership of this Pastor helped me to understand what it meant to have a true relationship with God. The Word was taught and realistic examples of navigating life were provided. Coming from a church where the majority of the members were your elders to going to a congregation that was full of people my age and on fire for God was amazing and refreshing.

We were both very active in the church and often served together. When it came time to make the decision to end our marriage, he went to leaders in the church and told them what was going on. I'm not sure if it was truly for guidance or to play the victim. I didn't feel the need to broadcast our issues and had a select few close friends in the church that I told. I knew these people would pray me through this situation unbiased about the outcome. Peter seemed to talk to anyone who would listen. One minister in particular told him he shouldn't leave no matter how many times I asked.

This hurt me because of who it came from. The ministry leader was someone that I went to college with and we worked in the college ministry together. It was hard to believe that they would say that to him and not converse with me throughout the whole process. A different minister at the church who would occasionally check in with me to see how I was faring. I never felt they truly took a side which made the other person's guidance feel like a slap in the face. There was also that one church member who tried to convince me to change my mind, to the point that it felt like I was being bullied into staying in my marriage. They would spend the majority of our conversations talking about how great of a person Peter was and how far he's come and the different things that he's been able to overcome health-wise. All I could think was, "Why are we having this conversation?"

I don't like disappointing anyone, which is another reason I stayed in this relationship way longer than I needed to. I felt like I let God down by saying I no longer wanted this marriage. Not wanting to let others down and self-guilt have been a personal struggle for years. I developed a pattern of relying more on my abilities instead of embracing God's possibilities. This is an area of continuing growth that I'm working on, so that I'm able to fully put my trust in God. Even now, after relocating I've struggled with being able to connect with a church body. I'm currently attending a great church, but it's not where I'm supposed to be planted. It's providing the spiritual covering I need until I can find a church home. The last thing I want to do is encounter a system that notices an unhealthy marriage but encourages it to continue without any help.

Guilt shadowed me for a long time about my decision. Despite the lack of support from Peter, I still thought I had to be present for him. Years of manipulation and gaslighting made me feel I had to be present for him. When we made the decision to start the separation process, *he* was the one to bring the subject up. He opened the door not realizing I would actually go through it. I actually felt I could get out this time.

In the year 2018 I began thinking about how I was going to remain in this marriage. It became a yearly thought. I called it the "Annual State of the Marriage". We would sit down and have a conversation about what we needed from each other, how we felt things were going and expressed any qualms to each other. I remember telling him I wasn't happy with examples. I wasn't looking for him to make me happy, that can only come from within. I felt like he didn't understand who I was. He would only view our marriage from the rose color glasses he wore. I often wondered if I good enough to make a marriage work? I was willing to doing my part but adjustments had to be made if we were going to last.

We did couples counseling with my mom's pastor; someone outside of our church. He is a great man of God and provided us with a lot of insight. We'd tried counseling at our church a few years before but that was a joke. We weren't heard and it was not a supportive experience. My mother's Pastor told us there was hope. I asked, "What do you mean by that?" His response was if we wanted to work on our marriage, we could make it work. But if we were ready to be done with it, he could see that happening as well.

Even with such a neutral answer, I made the decision to remain in my marriage. No one told me I had to stay, that was my decision. I was trying to prove to myself that I was capable to being a wife. I was also concerned about what the church would say. Divorce in the church is often frowned upon. My supports from church let me know that everything was going to be ok. We weren't the first couple to divorce, and we wouldn't be the last couple.

Navigating being separated while still living with a spouse is not for the faint of heart. In North Carolina, couples must live in completely separate households before being eligible for a divorce. Financially he couldn't get out on his own. We decided to live "separately" while remaining in the home together for a year and then file for divorce. That was good in theory, but didn't work out too well. He still viewed us as a married couple because things carried on like normal; this was my mistake. I continued to cook for him and made sure he had what he needed. One of his family members said during a phone conversation, "I hope Cathy ain't cooking for you because I wouldn't be cooking for you." He was offended by that statement. I laughed so hard on the inside. Being a married woman was part of my identity and even though things were bad, it felt loss without that title. I clung to it so closely that I didn't know how to separate myself. Even though he wasn't always deserving, I still honored that role.

One time I went out of town for a little get away, I just packed my bags and left. No word to him about where I was going or when I was coming back. Upon my return he had a fit like a toddler, he was big mad. I tried to explain that if we were living separate, he wouldn't even know that I was gone. My thoughts were if we're living as separate individuals, then he don't need to know my comings and goings. He no longer had access to that part of me.

Well, he changed his tune when he recognized that I was making efforts to live my life without him. When this process started, he was on board with us separating. He shared with me that he felt the marriage had been over years ago, but he wanted to see how far we could go. Now his decision was changing and wanted us to reconsider getting a divorce and start over being friends. He wanted to work things out now. This is from the same man who told me he knew the marriage was over years ago but didn't feel the need to do anything different.

I didn't know who Cathy was anymore. I lost the essence of her over the years. But I knew I'd reached my breaking point. Even while we were living as separate, he was working, but still the majority of the bills fell on me. He would help out occasionally with maybe the light bill or something, but everything else still fell to me. Although it was frustrating, it felt easier because we also needed that financial separation. My hope was for him to begin stacking his money so he could afford to move out when the time came.

It eventually got to the point where I wasn't sleeping well. Insomnia set in. My performance at work was impacted and I knew something had to give. I don't recommend living in a shared home while trying to separate at the same time. It does not work. Zero out of ten recommendation. My goal was to file for an absolute divorce, and this could be done without an attorney, but I eventually had to retain one because I couldn't trust that Peter would go through with the stated plan. Our separation clock reset when he eventually moved out.

The catalyst to finally get him to see that I meant business, and lit a fire under his feet was when I broke away from performing those wifely duties. I did everything solely for Cathy. No cooking enough for him, no checking in on him to see how he was doing because at that point, I really didn't care. He had breath in his body. He was living. He was fine. He didn't need me to check in on him. A member of my writing tribe, I believe it was Lissa, suggested that I stop cooking. There were other suggestions to cut the internet and other things, but when I stopped *cooking* for him, that was the nail in the coffin.

God blessed me with tons of support during this time that helped bring about this change. I was active in a writing tribe, working on my first novel and shared with them what I was dealing with. Their support was amazing I received was amazing. Tribe, along with my family and close friends provided the support I needed to stand up against what felt like a giant in my life. I stopped asking him if he needed assistance with anything. I pulled back on the level of support that I had provided him. He would ask me, "Why are you acting cold like you don't like me or that you don't love me". I let him know that I still loved him, but I didn't like him anymore.

It took a while, but I finally understood that all the different times I had been manipulated by him to remain in this marriage were because it benefited him more than it benefited me. Yes, I have to wash my own clothes now. I still hate it, but I can get it done. When I started washing my own clothes, again you would have thought I punched him in the stomach. But I realized, by allowing him to continue to wash my clothes, it gave him hope that we were going to go back to the status quo. When I started moving differently, started taking on my own responsibilities, not checking in with him to make sure he was okay or catering to him, he realized, this isn't the environment that he wanted to be in. And it put a little fire under him.

The weekend he moved out, I took myself to the beach. The beach is my happy place. And I spent all day just being one with nature, but I was also allowing the stress of the last few years begin to drain away. When I came back, his boxes were packed and stacked up in the garage. I thought I was just happy to be home. No, I was excited to see those boxes. This is *actually happening*. In the midst of this separation, I was still dealing with the grief of my mother's death.

Whether he realized it or not, my mom living with us was part of the reason we stayed together for those last few years. And not that she was pushing me to stay because she always said, "Do whatever you feel is going to be necessary for you, I got your back either way". I wanted my mom to have peace in our home and didn't want her to feel uncomfortable or in the way because me and Peter weren't getting along. There was a special grace my mother had on her life and to have her our proximity connected us to the blessing.

Therapy was an intricate part of my healing. My therapist was sent by God. She helped me believe that I could get through this trial. At the beginning of my therapy, I thought, "Oh, it's just grief. My thought was "Everyone can use some support during grief". But she helped me realize that I was depressed. I started having days that getting out of bed was a chore and showering became an option. I would have to tell myself "*Go put some water on your ass. Get your ass up!*" I had use positive self-talk and encourage myself. Working in the mental health field and also dealing with mental health issues, was something that I had to wrap my mind around. Just because I have helped people for close to twenty years, that didn't make immune me to needing help myself.

I talked with my therapist about medication as I was on the fence about taking that step. I was consistent with our sessions and doing the work, but something was off. She encouraged me to reach out to my primary doctor and to discuss what was going on. I dragged my feet but I called and got an appointment with my doctor. I eventually did start taking medication. I'm so glad that I made the decision to take medication. I felt myself come back. I remember watching something on television, and I laughed one of those deep down, truly joyous laughs. It scared me because I hadn't heard myself have a good genuine laugh in what felt like years. That was a wakeup call for me.

It's like, "Girl, do you realize how far you have come?" And that was my motivation to just be okay and tell myself, "I can do this". I can live without being a wife. I can live as Cathy. My marching orders were to find out who I am and to begin that journey not allow fear to hold me back or keep me paralyzed. I know we are told not to walk in fear. But yes, it happens. Fear had consumed me to a certain degree. I'm finally beginning to break through and not allowing it to dictate what my life was going to be like. Fear no longer has a place in my life.

Getting a divorce was one of the best decisions I could have made for myself. I didn't physically hurt him or talk down about him, but I simply protected my peace and adjusted my crown.

BLACK STEEL A POEM BY PAT G'ORGE-WALKER

Struggles, they attacked me
Though I had no permanent shape
They found me and when they did
I was thrust into a fire
And without my permission
I was shaped and hammered in that fire
Only to be quickly submerged in cool water

Often, certain blessings came upon me
And when I gave no thanks
Without a second thought, I was
Thrust again into the fire
Hammered and reshaped
Again, quickly submerged in cool waters

At an age where knowledge should have ruled me
Instead, I searched for more comfortable things
To use as my consequence, again into a fire
Chastised with life's repercussions and reshaped

Once more, then quickly submerged in cool waters

After repeated lessons, good and bad
After being consumed over and over in the fire
I became hard, impossible to break,
My spirit soared with invincibility

"Now I see" said my reason for being
Black Steel only comes about
After the thrusting in many fires
And the cooling off in many waters
I have arrived, I am ready for warfare
I am a supernatural weapon
I am God's Black Steel
Only to bend and to be used
by His Will

ABOUT THE AUTHORS

Mary Monroe is a *New York Times* bestselling African-American fiction author. Her first novel, The Upper Room, was published by St. Martin's Press in 1985. She is best known for her novel God Don't Like Ugly (originally published by Dafina Books in Fall 2000), and the series revolved around the characters first introduced in this book. Mary Monroe is the third of four children, born in Toxey, Alabama. She spent the first part of her life in Alabama and Ohio, moving to Richmond, California in 1973. Successful author and mother of two children, Mary currently resides in Oakland, where she continues to write bestselling novels.

Naleighna Kai is the USA TODAY, Essence®, national bestselling and award-winning author of several controversial novels that plumb the depth of unique love triangles or women's issues. She is also a contributor to a New York Times best-seller, one of AALBC's 100 Top Authors, a member of the Chicago Vocational School Hall of Fame (CVS), Mercedes Benz Mentor Award Nominee, and the E. Lynn Harris Author of Distinction. In addition to successfully cracking the code of landing a deal for herself and others with a major publishing house, she continues to "pay it forward" with the annual Cavalcade of Authors which gives readers intimate access to the most accomplished writing talent today.

Stephanie M. Freeman- is a #1 Bestselling Author, ghostwriter, developmental editor and publishing consultant, whose profes-sional writing career began back in 2012 when Crimson Romance, an imprint of Simon & Schuster, published her first novel, Necessary Evil. Since then, she has explored different writing genres including, Mysteries, Thrillers, Romantic Suspense and the Paranormal. Stephanie has amassed a loyal group of fans who eagerly await her latest releases. Her Diamonds, Blood and Shadows Series is a fan favorite. With multiple five-star reviews of her work, Stephanie M. Freeman continues to push literary boundaries.

Pat G'Orge-Walker is the Essence(R), national bestselling and award-winning author of the Christian fiction Sister Betty comedy series, as well as contemporary fiction, Women's issues, Romance novels. The novels published by Kensington/Dafina that fearlessly burrow into issues sometimes labeled taboo or left unsaid by Christian and secular community without subverting the Good News or watering down the potency of its message. She is also a contributor to New York Times anthologies and a three-time AALAS winner for Comedy as well as several other prestigious awards.

In a climate where personal development and entrepreneurship is now becoming "The American Dream", **La Ammitai** is committed to help guide others to their passions, purpose, and fulfill their most grand desires. La is a highly sought out Transformation Strategist, Master Numerologist, and #1 Best Selling Author. She utilizes numerology as the catalyst to leverage personal and professional success. Also specializing in NLP, inner child healing, law of attraction, and manifestation, she has transformed many lives in her unique approach to self-awareness. La believes that everything that one desires is an inside job. Her transparent, action-prone approach soars her client's to the best version of themselves.

Danielle Detiege, widely recognized as Coach Danni D, is a transformative Work with Ease Coach, dedicated public speaker, and engaging facilitator who empowers individuals to find clarity, purpose, and confidence. Drawing from over two decades of experience in Administration and Operations, and a deep understanding of psychology, Danielle uniquely blends strategic thinking with heartfelt guidance. Her personal journey, rooted in a

legacy of service from her social worker mother and a grandmother who "mothered everyone she met," fuels her passion for helping others. She is also a devoted wife to her high school sweetheart, proud mother to a brilliant son, and dog mom to Walter, her beloved "business partner."

Bridgett McGill is a math and science teacher in her eleventh year of education in Chicago Public Schools. Her passion for teaching and specifically teaching math was grounded in her own educational journey. She is also the award-winning author of "How Does Your Garden Grow - Cultivating a Life of Abundance," written in 2017. In 2019 she published the accompanying Interactive Journal. Bridgett is the founder of the Queen Within, an organization that focuses on women's empowerment and community development. This organization also has an online presence with more than 300 members. Women in this group appreciate a safe space and enjoy monthly activities and daily words of encouragement.

U.M. Hiram is a #1 Bestselling Author and Publishing Consultant. She is a human resource professional and a retired Navy veteran. Her love for writing began at an early age, evolving into independent publishing. She currently writes in multiple genres that include Christian fiction, contemporary romance, inspirational, paranormal, and romantic suspense. Reading, traveling, watching sports, and spending time with her family is what she enjoys doing the most when not putting pen to paper.

Randi Coley has a bachelor's in psychology and Maters of Health Science in Addictions studies. She is an addiction and mental counselor that has worked in the helping and social services field for 20 years. Her goal is to educate, inspire minister, motivate, and uplift by words of inspiration, mentoring, leadership and behavioral modification practices for change.

Yvonne Elliott is a talented author hailing from the city of Chicago. Her journey in the literary world has been nothing short of extraordinary. In 2022, Yvonne's debut memoir "Rebirth: Rising out of the Shadows and into the Light," took the world by storm. It soared to become Amazon #1 New Release and earned her the esteemed title of #1 Best Selling Author in not just one, but two categories. A remarkable achievement, indeed.

Cathy A. Brown lives in the triad area of North Carolina and is a graduate of East Carolina University. She grew up in a military household and lived in various parts of the United States, with Hawaii being the most memorable. Her love for reading began while at Nimitz Elementary School, trying to check out as many books as possible. Reading was an escape and allowed her to explore the world. As a licensed mental health and addiction counselor with over 20 years of experience, Cathy understands the importance of encouraging and supporting others at their lowest points in life. She loves to learn and travel; hoping to find new knowledge about the places she visits. Spending time with family and friends bring her joy. She wouldn't be the person she is today without their love and support.

Karen G. Stampley is a Licensed Certified Belief Therapist and Mindset Makeover Champion who empowers women who feel unfulfilled to unleash their "inner champion" by conquering limiting beliefs and negative thought patterns. Through her signature Five Steps of Faith Methodology, she helps women develop unshakable confidence and the kind of faith-in-action that leads to the deeper personal fulfillment they've long yearned for. She is the author of two powerful faith-based books—The Five Steps of Faith – The Ultimate Mindset Makeover and The Saboteur of Faith—and the visionary founder of E.Y.E. A.M. Empowerment Entity. With over 30 years of experience and a deep passion for seeing others walk in wholeness, Karen's heart beats to see women healed, equipped, and boldly aligned with their God-given identity and purpose.

THE MERRY HEARTS
INSPIRATIONAL SERIES

Some use God's word to justify domestic violence, imprisonment, slavery, and systematic racism rather than preach peace, joy, salvation, and love. Throughout the Merry Hearts Inspirational series, readers will experience scripture as never before. Authors take one-dimensional Biblical characters and breathe new life into them to become relevant for the reader.

Over time, many things have been misinterpreted, but the one important thing is that God's grace isn't just for men. Christ valued women so much. He had His most profound conversations with women. Christ performed astounding miracles through them, and following His resurrection, He appeared to the women first.

Throughout scripture, God's love for women and everyone-no matter ethnic background or gender-may be found, from Genesis to Revelation. May you come to know His love in an authentic, tangible way.

Each book in the Merry Hearts Series is a standalone and can be read in any order:

Book 1 – Journey – Lisa Dodson [Ruth and Boaz]

Book 2 – Visions– J. L. Campbell [The Outside Child]

Book 3 – Purpose – Florenza Denise Lee [The Unnamed Woman]

Book 4 – Growth - Janice Allen [Esther, The Three Hebrew Boys}

Book 5 – Transition -- Naleighna Kai [The Levite's Concubine]

Book 6 – Choices – Pat G'Orge-Walker [The Faithful Wife]

Book 7 – Patience – Terri Ann Johnson [Moses]

Book 8 – Persistence – U. M. Hiram [Hannah, The Centurion]

Book 9 – Transformation – Naleighna Kai [Tamar and Amnon]

THE GRATEFUL HEARTS
INSPIRATIONAL SERIES

Betrayal is a bitter pill chased with forgiveness.

The snow was falling, and Stephanie M. Freeman was dying. A brutal attack left her with a lifetime of heartbreak and scars. Trusting others with the unspeakable made her trauma worse. Februarys are hard for her, but a promise kept, and an unlikely group of strangers reminded her of a simple, yet profound truth.

Stephaniemfreemanauthor.com

Give up one year of your life and it will change you forever ...

Standing on the edge of adulthood, J. L. Woodson had a choice. A hard, fast 'no' meant staying in the comfort zone. Saying 'yes' would take him on a journey beyond all of his hopes and dreams.

Two men from different moments in time heeded a call and turned their pain into their purpose.

Just as Noah shared his salvation with his children; parents and teens will grow the most by experiencing this story together.

Visit www.nktribecalledsuccess.com

30 DAYS OF ME

This transformational self-development book utilizes numerology and other techniques that will help you self-identify, connect with your inner-self, process buried emotions, and reflect on profound lessons that life has been teaching you all along through your past and present circumstances. This book is designed to help you:

· Become more self-aware
   · Learn how to set better boundaries
   · Learn how to forgive yourself and others
   · Learn how to own your energy and stand in your power
… and most of all, how to love yourself as a whole being without the need for validation from outside sources.

You've invested enough time and energy into everything else. It's time to take the journey of you, with 30 Days of Me.

Authorlaammitai.com

CULTIVATING A LIFE OF ABUNDANCE

"If you compared your life to a garden right now, right today, what would you find? Is it flourishing, lush and full; are there a few green spots here and some brown patches there, or is it depleted because you've given everything away?

We have to ask ourselves every day: What does my garden need? Does it need the sun of encouragement; could it benefit from the fertilizer of forgiveness; would the pruning of confession bring great relief, or is it simply craving the beauty of rest?

As we walk through the gardens of our lives, we will find that we have within us, all we need to cultivate a life of abundance; we only have to be still, listen and let the beauty come forth."

THE FIVE STEPS OF FAITH

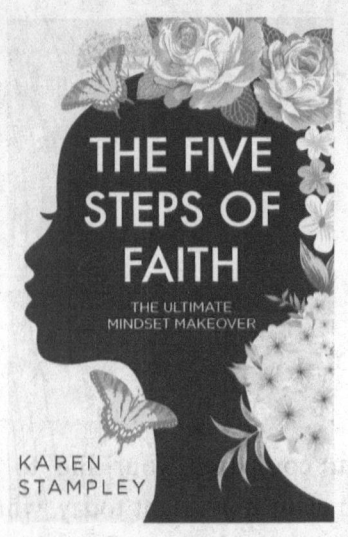

The 5 steps of Faith and its action steps are the building blocks that helps you to establish fundamental growth, stability and productive ELEVATED thinking patterns as well as developing a Spiritually Aligned Belief System.

Mindset Makeover using the "5 steps of Faith" is a vital tool that can be applied in every area of your life. With Faith and consistency the rewards can be revolutionary.

You are equipped to recognize, resist then shift from the old negative thought patterns and critical self talk replacing them with the Spiritual truth. Your new Elevated Faith Mindset empowers you to reach your goals and dreams while embracing your new Authentic self!

Find out more:

Eyeamvictory.com